CU00538912

Pips and Pipping

HOW WE MAKE OURSELVES SMALLER
AND WHAT TO DO ABOUT IT

by Per Schiøttz with
with Keith Scott-Mumby MD

Copy and Share This Book

This book is Copyright © 2019 by Supernoetics® Inc. ALL RIGHTS RESERVED, published by Supernoetics® Inc. an imprint of Mother Whale Inc. PO Box 19452, Reno, Nevada, 89511, USA, with permission from authors Per Schiøttz and Keith Scott-Mumby MD.

www.supernoetics.com

ISBN: 978-0-9968786-2-3

The text of this book is licensed under the CREATIVE COMMONS SHARE ALIKE LICENSE. More information about this license is available at:

http://creativecommons.org/licenses/by-sa/3.0/us

The book remains copyright of the authors and Supernoetics® Inc and may NOT be used without full attribution.

The "Freedom Tools" material is distributed in the hope that it will be useful but without any warranty, expressed or implied, as to its merchantability or fitness for a particular purpose. Use it at your own risk. See the applicable licenses for more details.

The marks Supernoetics®, Punk Psychology®, Hypnoetics™, and "Working for the purposeful re-invention of Mankind®" are trademarks belonging to Keith Scott-Mumby and may only be used with permission. Permission is automatically granted to copy them in any complete verbatim copies and translations of this work.

Copies have been sent for registration with the US Library of Congress.

Disclaimer

This book is a work of education, entertainment and life experience. It is not to be construed as medical, psychiatric or clinical psychology technique, unless used by a licensed MD or clinical psychologist.

Content is merely suggestions and the experience of one man. There is no guarantee that these observations and practices will apply to every person.

You use the content entirely at your own risk.

We cannot accept responsibility for changes that occur in your life, or the lives of those around you, whether problematic, or bursting into love, joy and success!

Table of Contents

In Memoriam

This work is dedicated, in memoriam, to a friend and mentor of exceptional wisdom and humanity:
Per Schiøttz 1939 – 2018.
Naval architect, shipwright, shipbuilding engineer, artist, model maker extraordinaire and "quality of life" coach!

Foreword: Understanding PIPs and PIPPING!

This foreword is based on a chapter in one of my own books, read and approved by Per Schiøttz. It is followed by all the extant pipping materials written by Per, who created his unique "Freedom Tools" experience, plus a short section written specially by me: Cultural Pipping. [Keith Scott-Mumby. Editor]

You are asked to refer to the glossary of terms, every time you come to an unfamiliar or jargon (special) word. The glossary is found at the end of this text.

Men and women everywhere live way below their potential. It's almost a maxim. You can see them as shrunken or shrivelled individuals. Why is that?

The extraordinary thing is that, in virtually EVERY case, the person is doing it to him or herself. The real cause is not what some outside influence is doing but the person agreeing to the outside influence.

This is astonishing of course. But it's also a positive thing, meaning that the person can reverse that, with a few simple, swift strokes. This chapter will show you how to get back your grander, more powerful self! Would that be important to you?

I'm talking about a phenomenon we call "pips" and "pipping". A person chooses to make him or herself smaller. The result is a loss of stature and freedom. We are "pipped" or crushed. He or she is living in a collapsed world.

Our good friend and senior life coach (pilot) Per Schiøttz has evolved a timely and fully satisfactory solution to this overall difficulty we call pipping. Let me explain...

It starts with people who are oppressive to others; crushers, if you like (not an official term). There is a very small percentage of people who seem to operate on the view that in order for them to get what they want, other people have to lose. They want "freedom" but at the expense of other people.

As Per reminds us often: *freedom is a quality, not a quantity*. But these crushers seem to think it's the other way round: there is only so much freedom and they grab as much as they can for themselves, at the expense of others.

This is the kind of individual you will find pulling others down:

You're no good.

You'll never amount to anything.

Step out that door and I'll see you regret it for the rest of your life...

Ha ha, loser!

You can expand this list of gibes infinitely from your own experience.

Such people may have various labels from the medical world: psychopath, sociopath, narcissist, borderline, etc. Overall, I refer to such individuals as "adverse personality types" (see Appendix 2). Often noone has spotted them or their destructive tendencies and such people go about their mischief unrecognized, unlabeled and unchecked.

The luckless individual under their influence often becomes wild and unstable, in fact a kind of borderline personality disorder case. He or she has difficulty freeing themselves from the malign influence and so, usually, he or she cannot hold onto case gain and freedom.

It starts early, sometimes, with a frenetic and dysfunctional parent, teaching the child rage, fear, misery and worthlessness. It continues with bullying at school. Shame in teenage years. And being low in the pecking order in adult corporate life.

Yes sir, being pipped is no fun and it can last a lifetime, unless someone knows how to use the "Freedom Tools"!

The crucial key is to shed the victim thinking. Everywhere in life, we are taught that bad things happen to us; people are mean; they try to crush you for their own gain; if you're smart, you dodge the bullet, but basically life is a bitch and others want you weakened or out of the way.

But it's not really like that. *No-one can hurt you, unless you play the game.* The bully has no effect at all, unless his or her victim decides to accept that they are weak and small. The bully relies on this computation, of course. People fold and crumble. But if you stand up to them, they are the ones who turn out to have no real power. Early on at school, I stood up to a guy at school who was making my life a misery. I finally flipped and beat the crap out of him.

Of course, I got punished as the perpetrator: teacher gave me a detention and sent me home, where my Mum gave me a beating for being bad! But it was worth it: the other kid never bothered me again. More to the point, I found myself to be better than a weakling. Thing is, I could not have been bullied by him, unless I had first made the decision he was stronger than me and I should be afraid. I "pipped" myself, by giving the bully the power.

It's YOUR Choice!

So there is a rule here, worth repeating: *nothing and nobody can hurt you, unless you go into victim mode and agree to it.* A "pip" has to reach a moment when he or she decides to make him- or herself weak or smaller. From then on, it's hurting mode. But it is the pip's own decision, really. Playing victim is silly and a loser's game (literally)!

Per Schiøttz's brilliant Freedom Tools, on which this booklet is based, are all about finding and re-engineering those defining moments when you decided to cave in to others. The path to recovery—freedom—is to dump the decision you took to make yourself smaller or accept another's point of view against your own. As you gain insight and shift, naturally, you quit doing it to yourself! The person undergoing this "cleansing" wakes up and comes alive. It's marvelous to see!

Another key learning: I have just described this phenomenon in terms of nasty, aggressive people, who seize your rights and your space, to make you shrink. But it is important to realize anybody can have that effect on you, if you allow it. Even a nice and intelligent person, who is merely strong-minded or forceful in his or her opinions, can end up creating pips.

That doesn't make strong-willed people bad! Just powerful in their effects on others!

If you adopt another's point of view or opinions, you are pipped, simply because they are not your own opinions. Do you see that? It doesn't even matter that the strong individual may be quite correct. He or she has been elected as the reason for abandoning your own point of view and the mechanism kicks in accordingly. So, the target for correction is rightly the pip, NOT the person who is dominating.

A lot of wasted psychology centers around the idea that the client was a victim. Bad things "happened to" him or her. You poor thing. So your husband was a brute? Your father abused you? Oh my God! She did WHAT to you? Kind of crap.

It's disempowering because it doesn't provide any role for the person in his or her own miseries. It's also a wrong indication, or big misownership, to ignore what the individual did to create their own problems. Yes, the husband may or may not have been unfaithful—but what did YOU do wrong or fail to provide, that he was ultimately discontented?

Why didn't you talk about it long ago, before things got out of hand. Did you actually listen to what your husband was saying years before and deal with it in some way? No? OK, you lose.

Even with the subject of bullies and brutes, you have to ask: why didn't the wife just walk out, instead of staying around to be "abused"? It's a core precept of the Freedom Tools writings that you cannot be free while you think nasty people do nasty things to you and hurt you. Yes, nasty people do bad things, but it only hurts you if you let it into your life, that's your fault, not theirs.

So we re-instate a person at cause. You cooperated with the domination, so YOU are the one who has to un-create the mess. A client must be brought up to the realization that domination, or what used to be called "suppression", is something you agree to—otherwise it doesn't exist. It's just water off a duck's back, as we say.

This goes wider in psychology. Bad happenings, stress, PTSD and a whole host of "causes" of misery have to be bought into, in order for them to take effect.

OK, so there are extreme dominators or bullies. You can't reason with them. We don't just "fix" it. We need to get the client out of harm's way. That may mean walking out, to put a stop to a bad situation. That's still putting the client at cause, not leaving him or her at effect.

YOU need to fix this is the real message, not complain about someone else, make wrong, victim, etc.

There are no witch hunts here! Unlike the abusive and discredited Scientology suppressive persons model, we do not seek disconnection from anybody. There is no need to break up families. That's misguided and, actually, stupid because it's missing the truth.

Cutting all connection with someone dominating can only have a temporary effect, if any. The real change comes when the pip stops shrinking and being a victim.

What the pip has to do, in effect, is disconnect from the burden they have taken on from the dominant person. That's an internal transition. You don't need to make a big deal out of it. It's just like snipping a cord!

Exactly how we do this is covered in Per Schiøttz's Freedom Tools, which follow this foreword. Anyone can study these tools. We only ask that you team up with a certified Freedom Coach, to make sure you don't vary, or step outside of, the procedure. This is not to be controlling but to make sure you get the amazing results!

Who Would Benefit From The Freedom Tools?

The answer is everybody. It's always good to resolve mental trash and get it cleaned up! It can be very empowering at times.

But some people need it more than others. Strong clues that a person has been chronically pipped would include the following:

- Your spouse always gets his or her own way.
- Domineering parents
- You were unhappy at school and felt bullied
- You were mocked and belittled while you were growing up
- In your career you always felt out of it and failed to get your own way
- Your view of things was often rejected or sneered at
- Person is making him/her self smaller in relationships

The important point to thoroughly grasp is that freedom is a quality; not a quantity. Most people are seeking freedom "from" certain restraints. The irony is that they have bought into the restraints. The answer to that kind of freedom lies within! Change your view; get rid of the restraints!

Freedom really means freedom "to"; to do what you will or have what you want. That's worthwhile freedom. It is not mindless lack of restraint, such as narcissism or borderline psychosis.

To achieve that highly desirable kind of freedom, a person must be free to think their own thoughts. One cannot be free, in any sense, if we buy into the opinions of others and accept their view as fact (*Fact:* something which can be proven to exist by visual evidence. *Opinion:* something which might or might not be based on a fact).

Pipping

All relationships have a degree of give and take. Sometimes one person may be a bit forgetful and take rather more than is given! But only when it's persistent and becoming a behavior pattern is it likely to be real domination. It's not just a question of one person getting persistent in making demands; the other person or persons have to serve these demands, for them to become anything like damaging. So, as the old saying goes, "It takes two to tango".

When this becomes serious is when one member of a partnership or group becomes seriously demanding and insisting on their own point of view all the time, without respecting or serving the needs of others. Gradually, he or she can slip into the role of being a dominator, while others create this effect by succumbing to the demands of the dominator.

When that stage is reached, the submissive partner (or group members) lose out by not being able to assert their own viewpoints or needs. Then it gets toxic. The losers (pips or dominated) have surrendered their freedom because they can't/don't get what they want. It goes to the dominators demands every time.

Eventually choosing to acquiesce always (because it's easier or for peace and quiet) means the pip has fewer and fewer options available. They have surrendered their freedom. The dominator has grabbed it, since it's on offer!

So a person who is one of a group of school friends might feel inferior, because he is always being scoffed at and his suggestions for a good time are ignored, gradually will become a slave/servant type figure to the group. He always follows their suggestions and suppresses his own desires. He is "pipped". He has consciously chosen to make himself smaller and less important.

Another example from school days would be a scholar who the teacher has taken a dislike to and starts to abuse verbally, calling him or her an idiot, a fool or implying he/she is not as competent or clever as the other students. This leads to that scholar being ostracized. The other kids follow the teachers line and treat him or her as someone inferior. To maintain some semblance of friendship and belonging, he or she puts up with the mistreatment and jibes. But is very unhappy. He or she would not have the freedom to BE self, fully expressed, or DO whatever he or she most desired.

This is just a simple example. But actually we lead very complex lives, bombarded by a wall of hurtful words and implications. TV ads shout that, unless you drive the right car, no girl will look at you. Or unless you wear the right kind of cosmetics, no man will take your seriously or find you sexy.

Friends, family and work colleagues are constantly making clumsy or diminishing remarks—not necessarily intentionally—but the effect is the same. By accepting another's viewpoint, we grow less in doing so.

People who actively work on enforcing their opinions onto others could be called dominating, but the person having opinions forced onto him is the one who makes himself smaller, no one else can.

Ultimately, it becomes a case of loss of identity, living to a high degree for others and by other people's opinions causing one's own personality to disappear. We all do, or have done this to a greater or lesser degree depending on who the other person is. Parents and peers are a very powerful influence in this respect.

The more we choose to obey other's opinions, commands and orders and take into ourselves another's characteristics, behavior patterns, ideas and thoughts, the less free an individual we will be; the more we lose our integrity. Eventually, the pipped person will listen less and less to his or her own inner dialogue, intuition and feelings. This will eventually lead to self-denial, self-hatred and self-defeating attitudes, all of which add up to less freedom.

The Chain

You will readily see that the term "pip" is appropriate, meaning a spot or insignificant speck!

Unfortunately, it becomes a chain reaction. The pip eventually takes on so much of the dominator's personality that he or she too becomes dominating or manipulative. The pip creates more pips; sub-pips, if you like.

Pips are slighter persons and operate closer to the emotion of fear than bullying and pushing people around. But that often makes pips quite treacherous and difficult to deal with. It is easy to be blinded by their seemingly mild front and complaints that *other people* are hurting *them*.

Just be careful what you buy into with these birds! All I know is when you remove the pipping, he or she will become nice, charming and contributive citizens, with a genuine concern for others.

Who Owns It?

Per Schiøttz reminds us that everyone has an ethical philosophy or codex which they live by. It's a person's "rules" or guidelines for what is OK to do in life. It could be "I will not engage in shoplifting" or "I'm OK and have a right to be here". These rules are more or less known to the person consciously. If the ethical codex contains: "I will listen to others opinions and then carefully consider if they shall be mine too", then you have a chance to not blindly accept other's opinions, perceptions and imperatives, etc.

In fact the burden of other people's thoughts, ideas and beliefs is a major problem in our human psyche. We are gregarious beasts, meaning herd animals. We tend to share and intermingle, till it becomes difficult to know whose is what. In fact we are now sufficiently aware of this consensus mode of thinking, that we have terms for it, like "memes" (thought viruses), "group mind" and the morphic resonance field.

This becomes massively important in self-growth work, personal coaching or therapy. It is extremely important that you are very sure that it is your own ideas, thoughts and behavior patterns that you start changing (transforming). If it really is other's opinions and ideas, which you have taken on, then it's a waste of time.

There is only one way to handle impositions from without, from an overbearing influence: cut the cord!

If Alice feels dominated by her mother, who says: "You are quite ugly", then that is the mother's opinion, not Alice's own. She must therefore CUT the connection to that opinion and realize that it is not hers and "send it back to the mother" right here and now.

Note carefully that she doesn't cut the connection to her mother; that would violate the universal solvent of all problems: Communication!!

There could be a small danger here, namely if you disconnect from something which IS your own. Then you will never get it fixed properly, as you believe it isn't yours and have disconnected from it, yet you were the one that created the little dysfunctional vortex. But this very small danger is not difficult to get around as soon as you get a little practice in this.

Procedure (For Self Or Clients)

1. First you must realize which persons, groups, places or situations etc. you feel have caused you to make yourself smaller. For each of them in turn, you write down all the different ideas, thoughts, behavior patterns, commands, unethical actions, opinions etc. picked up from that person or group or in that situation.

2. Then in your own universe you actually cut (sever) the connection to these items, realizing it's not yours and seeing whose it is at the same time. If you come across something you have already disconnected from earlier, just acknowledge that.

3. Finally you sign this "document" that you have actually disconnected from these things.

The whole action can take several hours or weeks or months depending on the client's case shape, but it is extremely important to do it very early in quality-of-life coaching, if not as the very first action.

Why?

When all this is done, the former-pip should figure out what rule has been missing from his or her written or unwritten ethical codex, which resulted in unwillingly adopting another's point of view. He or she should write it down as an addition to his or her ethical code. If this is kept in times to come (eternal Nows) then it will act as a guarantee that the pip will never again allow his or her freedom to be lessened or taken away.

Here is an example of a handling Peter did regarding his father. It's a very ordinary example, from a situation which is very common:

I, Peter Hansen, do hereby cut the connection to my father's:

1. *Insults and invalidation by saying I am stupid.*
2. *Talking badly about me to my friends.*
3. *Attempts to decide:*
    a. *My education*
    b. *How to spend MY money*
    c. *With whom I can date*
    d. *My hairstyle*
    e. *Which books I should read*
    f. *When to go to bed*
4. *Lack of communication.*

I realize that these are my father's and not my characteristics

Signed
Peter Hansen

When this is done for all items, you should experience more freedom and a growth as a person, again depending on state of case. The most incredible results have occurred with this handling, including the "dominator" becoming suddenly warm and friendly towards the client.

If there is no change or not a lot of growth, then there are still unhandled items or you have disconnected from something which is yours. The ability to "separate" can be very low in the beginning. Don't fret. Your skills will grow.

It picks up pretty quickly and in the end the client will stay un-pipped with constantly expanding freedom as THE result.

Plus there is a "secret" step, called personality de-mixing, which makes sense of it all. You get that with the full materials when you enroll. And did I say: it's FREE to learn?

We are engaged in the purposeful re-invention of Mankind®. Sharing this topic is a great place to start!

OK, what follows is a text written by the late Per Schiøttz and lightly edited. Per's English was remarkably good and he will always be missed for his sunny and wise personality.

For many a day, we discussed (argued almost) about what terms to use. For years, I had been using pips and "pipping" but Per thought it was bad practice to use labels for people. Yet he kept using terms like the "suppressor" and the "dominator" and I pointed this out. However I could see his viewpoint: the label was not very important; it was the mechanism that was crucial to a person's recovery and growth.

Eventually, he reluctantly came round to my use of the term "pip", which actually does hold a lot of information. It paints a picture of the shrunken individual who gives him or herself very little space on the map of their own ecosystem!

The so-called "Freedom Tools" remain, throughout, Per's invention and I am delighted to help spread their value and meaning.

Copyright © Keith Scott-Mumby 2019 ALL RIGHTS RESERVED

1. Capaciousness

Before proceeding with more theory and practice, it is important to understand a key concept: capaciousness of mind. What does that mean? It's a version of tolerance. Take a look at figure 1...

Fig 1 Capaciousness

Here you see a person with sufficient generosity of mind—capaciousness—that he or she can take on board other ideas, without surrendering his or her own viewpoint. This is as it should be.

So, if one person thinks the Earth is flat, and somebody else comes along with the viewpoint that it is round as a ball, then a capacious person will be able to encompass this new, foreign, and very strange viewpoint.

The two viewpoints can now be evaluated in relation to each other, particularly if they contain data of comparable magnitude. (The idea that the Earth is flat can be compared to the idea that it is spherical, but not with the idea that "I know best" or "carrots are healthy"). When they are being evaluated and compared and embraced there is a possibility of learning something new, and of understanding the new stuff, and realizing what it encompasses and implies.

That's Figure 1.

In a real-life example, one's own viewpoint could be "I am a polite person and treat people well" and suddenly the wife or a friend says: "You are very rude a lot of the time. You have insulted me frequently". If there is room for that other viewpoint, meaning there is capaciousness, then there is a chance of evaluating the two viewpoints in relation to each other and improving behavior.

But what if the person does not have the generous capacity for absorbing and integrating other people's ideas? One of two things will happen: either the person rejects any other view than their own (arrogance, dogma, rigidity); or the person's *own viewpoint* is negated and he or she is overwhelmed by the other person's ideas (pipping).

Fig 2 No room for new ideas. Not capacious

Figure 2 shows a person who isn't capacious, who doesn't have room for a new, different, foreign, or provocative viewpoint. He will promptly reject the new and different idea (B) - WITHOUT evaluating, analyzing, feeling, or in any other way sensing the other viewpoint. It is rejected immediately, because there is no room, it doesn't even enter his space – and that would be the first requirement for evaluating it.

It can be extremely frustrating to deal with a "type 2 – a non-capacious" person, if you really want to introduce him to new ways of doing things, something you KNOW will help him with what he is trying to accomplish. Maybe you actually have more experience with the subject than the other person. Any teacher has experienced this. Not until he gets the student to be willing to contain a new viewpoint in his space will the student be able, in any way, to learn something new.

You will often notice this in situations where it is taking a person an exorbitant amount of time to learn something new. The new information can be repeated again and again. At some point one might get lucky and repeat it at a time when the student is in suitably high spirits, where there is more room and more capaciousness. Suddenly it sinks in.

Capaciousness has appeared.

When studying something new, a lack of capaciousness can give problems that might not have been noticed before. A lack of capaciousness, which often shows itself as fixed or stuck ideas, won't make room for the new ideas that inevitably will surface when studying something new.

Fig 3. Pipped. Own viewpoint kicked out

Figure 3 shows the person who isn't capacious, but only has room for one viewpoint at a time. When a new viewpoint appears, he immediately rejects his own viewpoint and takes on the new one. The old viewpoint is rejected IMMEDIATELY. The new one is not evaluated, it is not being examined and analyzed or felt. It hasn't really been perceived.

He doesn't have room for two viewpoints, and he is so uncertain about the one he has, that he immediately rejects it in favor of the new viewpoint. This kind of person can seem very naive and easily controlled by authority.

If you are vacationing in a cabin without electricity, and you ask such a person to go and find the "kerosene vacuum cleaner", he will probably start looking for it immediately. His own viewpoint—that vacuum cleaners run on electricity, not on kerosene—gets rejected the moment you give him the idea of the kerosene vacuum cleaner. He will be very uncertain about his own views because of the very small, or totally lacking, capaciousness (this is a true-case example!)

He may seem like somebody who "learns" new things with lightening speed, but his understanding of those new things is found in a very small place. The new ideas are accepted with closed eyes, plugged ears, and an unfeeling rigidity. If you check his understanding he might be able to rattle off the accepted viewpoint, but he will not be able to use it for anything sensible since he hasn't understood it, examined it, or felt in his heart what it is about.

Capaciousness is obviously very important if one wants to learn new things. The inability to contain new viewpoints is the biggest barrier, also when it comes to the mutual understanding between people. If you can't contain any other viewpoint, how can you possibly contain a whole other person with many other viewpoints?

In marriages and other close relationships between people it often happens that a viewpoint can't be contained. The viewpoint is rejected by some kind of judgment: "That idea of yours is crazy", "You are crazy", "Do you really believe that yourself?"

If the different viewpoint is accepted and one's own viewpoint is rejected instantly because of lacking capaciousness, then the judgment will often be about oneself.

"My idea is crazy", "Where did I get that from, I better reject it immediately, or the others will think I am stupid", "Others are smarter than me", "I am stupid".

Here goes the self-denigration, the making self smaller, the true source of (self-caused) domination. Maybe, in a situation like this, there might not be a dominating person within miles - just an assumed dominator!

The How and The Why

When ideas are rejected without being felt or analyzed we often need a reason for it. We need an explanation, mostly for ourselves. Lack of room is not seen as a reason, so we invent reasons.

The rejection of new viewpoints from others can be explained with: "I know best", "Don't you think you are somebody", "Anything new is dangerous", etc., etc.

Own viewpoints can be rejected and the rejection is justified with: "I lack confidence", "I can't trust myself", "Nobody can understand my views", "Communication is of no avail".

So reader, how is your own capaciousness? Is it large? Do you find it very easy to make room for the viewpoints of others, or for your own? Are you listening to others' viewpoints? Are you listening? Are you interested?

Try to sense your own capaciousness over the next couple of days. Feel it. What happens when other viewpoints are impinging, trying to enter your space? What do you do with them? What do you do with your own viewpoints? Notice what is happening.

If you suddenly find yourself in a group where two or more people are talking at the same time you can be 100% certain that at least one person isn't listening. Who is it? Is it yourself? Are you interested, or are you trying to be interesting? Where is your capaciousness? Where is the other person's capaciousness?

Evaluating viewpoints, own or others', mainly consists of seeing differences, similarities and identical things. Sometimes this can be hard and another person's guidance (coaching) can be very beneficial. (See the chapter "How Can I Gain More Freedom".)

You can get much enjoyment out of observing your own capaciousness in relation to other people and other viewpoints. It will expand and get roomier simply because you start observing it. You notice it and it will be allowed to develop. There will be space for the capaciousness and then there probably aren't many more limits after that. Freedom is NOT a quantity even though some might want to persuade you about that. Freedom is a quality, a quality of viewpoint monitored by your capaciousness.

Try it !!

In Supernoetics®, we believe the ultimate gracious, intelligent—and actually POWERFUL—position to be in, is to be able to understand and tolerate all points of view, without rejection, argument, conflict and (especially) without violence. It takes grandness of Being to be able to do that. The person has to be, as we say, comfortable in their own skin. Happy to be "me"—and ultimately that is the meaning of Supernoetics®: "Me to The Max!" (Super: biggest, best, superior, and Noetics: mind and spirit).

So Supernoetics® is not just a body of data; it's a way of life!

2. Freedom and Domination

Our relationships are one of the most important factors for our quality of life. But relationships present the possibilities of disagreements, discussions, fights and wars on the one side – and affinity, empathy, love and togetherness on the other side. There is a positive and negative side. The positive being where the good relationships flourish; and the negative side is where we find disagreements, conflicts etc.

When there is conflict, some things are very obvious, at least when the conflict has gone solid and into war. On an international level you see very expensive and obvious war machines consisting of war ships, army trucks and tanks and fighter planes.

When there is no conflict, no war, no fighting, there is peace and quiet but that peace can actually be overlooked, as it doesn't make the news. There is freedom and nobody bothers to mess with others. Everybody is respected and has equal rights and the positive things mentioned above prevail.

When there is a conflict there is immediately also name calling. The enemy must have a name. There is an endless spate of pejorative names created for the opposition, the bad ones, the enemy, the bastards, suppressors, dominators, terminators, bullies, thugs, heathens, etc. etc. As soon as there is an agreement that so and so is a suppressor, then there is naturally also someone who is being suppressed, a victim, or at least someone who thinks he is being suppressed.

When you agree to that, you are being pipped. You are not fully aware of your environment, as you have to keep an eye on the suppressor all the time in order to not get surprised by the next attack (even though there may never be a next attack). Your attention gets fixed on the suppressor and will not be free.

To the extent you have your attention fixed onto another or others, to that extent you might potentially create problems, as you are not there 100 percent and doing what you are supposed to be doing. The controlling or abusive individuals we can call or consider "suppressors", "crushers" or "dominators". Pippers might make sense but we don't use that.

The point is this rag bag of people have many different attitudes, methods and motivations: The Good and The Bad, the Holy ones and the Sinners, Bullies and Victims, the Antisocial and the Social etc. etc.

People with negative characteristics can again be split up in different categories as per the severity of the hostility, domination or assumed domination they display. Some examples could be: strict parents, insecure bosses who got mad, colleges who try to bypass your advancement, thugs trying to secure their own positions, criminals who knock you down for winning's sake.

There ARE outright dominating persons, people who try to keep others down in order to further their own advancement and prosperity. They have some weird idea that freedom is limited, that everybody can't be free at the same time, that freedom is a quantity, not a quality (See chapter "Freedom is a Quality").

The hard core cases actively create conflicts and start fights and wars. These are the real trouble makers. They may be fighting you for no obvious reason. In some cases there is no rational reason because the reason they fight is NOT in the present, it lies in a long gone fight or battle they are still engaged in; it was never completed nor ended in a peaceful manner.

It could even be an old traumatic incident which really hurt, or it could be some old violent death in a past life. The old incident has been re-activated with all its pain and horror, to such an extent that it overwhelms the dominating person causing him to fight anyone and everyone in his environment who has the smallest amount of characteristics similar to those in the age old incident he is still fighting. He has problems in seeing differences, similarities and identical things.

If a person with similar characteristics to one in his old traumatic incident, appears, he doesn't see the similarities as such, but he sees them as identical and starts fighting. And if he doesn't see them his subconscious might react to them and a fight is started. He might fight, and even be very clever about it, but he doesn't know consciously why he is fighting and trying to dominate or suppress you.

The way out for this guy is of course to handle that old incident and get all the emotional charge and force and fixed ideas out of it. This is actually not very difficult to do for a coach who knows his business. But the "dominating person" might have reacted to a lot of similarities in people in many parts of his life. Therefore he can't see straight any more. He confuses friendly people with enemies. He doesn't realize what his reaction is based on, and therefore sees nothing wrong with himself.

As a consequence he does not typically show up for coaching. "I am OK, it's just all the other bastards who need to be kept down for my own freedom to prevail" – he might think. Actually deep down under the traumatic incidents from the past, he really is OK, and if you get him dug out from down there, you will find another lovely person who will be able to grant others the freedom to be, do and have - whatever they please to experience.

You may encounter two such persons meeting each other and a real conflict and war will start out. (Can you imagine: two dominating persons having to do a program together, both wanting to be the boss... disaster! You get a war between two tyrants).

He might also run into other people who are not in a similar situation, being affected by the past. But all the noise around the dominating person, his commands and orders, attitudes and behaviour patterns and fixed ideas make the other people buy into some of these things and knowingly or unknowingly adopt some of his (smart or unavoidable) characteristics and make them their own. They change into someone they were NOT before they met the dominating person. These people took the characteristics or ideas, including self-limiting beliefs, upon themselves in order to please the dominator or in order to survive or avoid some unpleasant consequences. Maybe they thought it was smart to do so.

Taking upon oneself others' characteristics will, whether they are good or bad, make you into something you are not. You will use energy to keep this condition going, and to the extent you do this, you have less power for your own endeavours. You have become less yourself. Some people have done this to such an extent that they can't see head nor tails in this personality mess and no longer know who they really are themselves. They made themselves smaller.

See chapter "How To Gain More Freedom" for the handling of this phenomenon.

Misownership

It is important to understand that the person who changed something in or about himself, for whatever reason, to adjust to the dominator, did it to himself. It was NOT the dominator who did it. The person made himself smaller. Brené Brown, research professor at the University of Houston, Texas, calls this "engineered smallness". It's deliberate.

The pip ended up being dominated by his own doing, with the dominator present and making a lot of noise.

Another, stronger person might not have done this, as he wouldn't care about the dominator's ideas and doings and attempts to dominate or boss him around etc. etc. He couldn't care less. Therefore the effects of a dominating personality are not an absolute, it is relative to the other or others around. Some will become dominated, some will not. Some will become affected, some will not. Some will sell out of their own power and integrity, some will not.

But we have all done this to ourselves, to a larger or smaller degree.

The full resolution of this is described in the chapter "How To Gain More Freedom". A handling is possible because the client was doing it by himself, to himself. You can only guide him and get him to change his mind about the characteristics he has taken from the assumed dominator. In fact it is enough for him to SEE that they are not his own characteristics, as they were not there before he met the assumed dominator. He just needs to stop using them, disconnect from them, send them back to the assumed dominator if need be. (A symbolic action of stopping the misownership, done mentally).

He will realise that he had mistakenly assumed that the other person was dominating him, whereas in fact, it was he who made himself be dominated. He made himself smaller because of an assumed domination. It was just another viewpoint or another person's ideas about something.

Correcting this misownership is what opens the door to a resolution. If the assumed dominator in your client's case was a real dominator, suppressing the hell out of your client you would not be able to handle it only by dealing with the client, but you would have to handle the dominator as mentioned above. (The dominator's traumatic incident).

If this is not possible, the assumed dominated person needs to re-evaluate his connection to the assumed dominator and with help from the coach become more causative in the relationship and the communication. He needs to know HOW to communicate and he needs to know from which level to communicate. Not only the technique of the communication is important, the quality of the communication is at least equally important.

Aggressive Assertive Communications

Dr. Jeremy Thompson has given a very good video on this. He explains the degrees of aggressive, assertive and passive communications and how to calm down and talk to an aggressive person. Here is the link to his illustrated speech: https://youtu.be/L3zj2gJXdTY or search YouYube.com for: "5 steps to better relationships using assertive communication."

It is very, very important to develop an awareness of what is going on between you and the people around you. What are they really saying when they talk to you, when the boss criticises you, when your wife evaluates something about you etc. etc.? They are generally dealing out opinions. You might agree with them and that is fine. But their ideas may also be different from your ideas. Sometimes they state facts, not opinions. (Fact being something we all agree on as we can all see it - like the sun going down).

Facts are fine, opinions have to be evaluated. Are they true for you or not? This is about capaciousness. If you take another person's opinion as a fact – for example, "The Earth is flat", as the common belief was once – you can create a lot of fear in sailors believing it, like the sailors getting into unknown waters believing they would spill over the edge of the Earth and disappear. If you on the other hand take facts as opinions, you might get hurt if you believe the fellow who tells you that you can drive a certain distance in two seconds flat... Bang...!

Opinions and facts, similarities, differences and identical things, misownership and ownership are all equally important words to know and use in all communication and relationships. It is important to be aware of these things as they are very instrumental in your experience of freedom. I guarantee you, that if all opinions are handled as opinions, facts are seen as facts, similarities, differences and identical things seen separately as such, you see what is your own stuff and not others' and vice versa, then you will experience a lot of freedom.

Study the rest of the book and you will know what I mean. You will also experience it, and you will be able to live and breathe freely if you work with this with a coach or do a workshop with these materials.

It will bring you a lot of free feeling and living!

Strangely, you will not feel the need to hit back at those who have overwhelmed and dominated you. In fact you will probably start to feel sorry for them. The poor things are so frightened by the need for "freedom", that their lives are truly miserable.

Even more astonishingly, the person who hurt you so much, made you feel threatened and caused you to make yourself smaller, will always change their attitude towards you, once you have gone through the Freedom Tools technique, honestly and comprehensively. So we don't seek to reject them; rather to bring them back to nurture. This is unique.

Disconnect from the "toxic" person is the watchword of weaker psychologies. It does not work well. The reason is simple: it puts the client at effect. "Poor you, see what they did to you?" Bad message.

So disconnection spreads hurt and dismay. It can only have a temporary effect when you take the person out of an area with heavy domination, but you still have to deal with the situation, sooner or later (or rather HE has to). Handling with the client as *effect* only, in my opinion and experience, makes the negative aspects more solid and he will not get out of it until he takes full responsibility as the person who really caused the pipping, and assumes cause.

With the new way of coaching presented here, it has become possible to handle these situations with the client as *cause*.

Many of my clients have proven this point with great clarity. No more proof is needed. There should be no more looking back. There is no more need to fear any of these so-called domineering, oppressive or suppressive persons. There is a way back - or forward if you will - to freedom again.

We are all members of energy cooperatives or "fields", meaning we are spiritually connected in groups by similar attitudes, ideas, experiences, etc. Rupert Sheldrake calls it the "morphic resonance" field.

If you handle a person's negative contribution to a field, the others, being connected to the same field, will lose the negativism too. The field will turn more positive. This is the reason that you will have the "dominator" of the "pipped" client respond to the client newly, but this time in a positive way.

This remarkable recovery is now available to anyone and everyone who wants to recreate the freedom, or rather to live in freedom once again, because freedom is the *natural* state, not being dominated. You are BIG. You are FREE. You are YOU...

3. How To Gain More Freedom

I have often heard the expression "Free me from this" and "Free me from that". If there really are a lot of things in a person's daily life he wants to be free *from* then he is guaranteed not to be a happy person. Freedom is not freedom FROM this or that or a whole lot of things. Freedom ought to be freedom TO do or be or have what you want.

Opinions and facts

In relationships, people often express an opinion about another person. The other person might take this opinion as a fact and thereby lose some of his freedom because the opinion was a limiting opinion. It becomes a limiting belief. For example, "It's dangerous to travel".

[Fact, one definition, there are several: A fact is something which can be proven to exist by visual evidence. Opinion: Something which might or might not be based on a fact].

Pipping

If dad tells Peter "You are quite stupid", and Peter somehow or other buys this, and later knowingly or unknowingly acts upon this, by for instance not taking the education he wants, then we are talking about self-invalidation, and Peter has lost some of the freedom he could have, at least in choosing education. Everybody is on a daily basis bombarded with others' opinions about this, that and the other.

People love to give good advice, and every time we connect to others' opinions and act accordingly (as if it were facts), which means we do not follow our own ideas, or listen also to ourselves, then we lose something of ourselves and become weaker and smaller. People who actively work at enforcing their opinions onto others could be called dominating, but the person having opinions and limiting beliefs forced onto him is the one who makes himself smaller by adopting them. No one else can.

The dominator has misunderstood something. He thinks that freedom is a quantity and therefore he has to keep others down in order to get the freedom for himself. Freedom is a *quality* – please!!

Integrity

Integrity means wholeness, all of it – without things missing, a condition where nothing has been removed nor corrupted or damaged. If a person has undamaged integrity then he hasn't given away any of himself. He exists in his wholeness as himself.

On the other hand, if he compromises his own honesty, his own wishes and perception of himself, then he loses integrity. If he adopts others' self-limiting beliefs and opinions about himself (un-examined) then he has given something of himself away. You could say that he has shrunk. He has become less himself. See Figure 1.

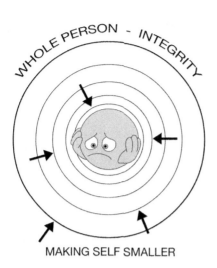

MAKING SELF SMALLER

Figure 1

Loss of identity

Some people live to a high degree for others and by other people's instructions and opinions, causing their own personality to shrink or disappear.

The more a person obeys others' opinions, commands and orders and takes onto himself others' characteristics, behavior patterns, ideas and thoughts, the less free he will be and the more he loses his integrity. He will listen less and less to his own convictions and values, his intuition and feelings. This will eventually end up in self-denial, self-hatred and self-defeating, which mean less freedom. We all do, or have done, this to a greater or lesser degree depending on who the other person was.

Ethics and Philosophy

Everyone has an ethical philosophy or code by which they live. It's their guidelines for what is OK to do in life. It could be "I will not en- gage in shoplifting" or "I'm OK and have a right to be here". These are more or less known to the person consciously. Loss of integrity and thus freedom is a result of lack of ethical philosophical codex. If the ethical codex contains: "I will listen to others opinions and then carefully consider if they shall be mine too", then you have a chance to not blindly accept others' commands, beliefs, opinions, perceptions etc., and lose integrity and freedom as a result.

Yours or mine?

If you want personal enhancement by for instance Personal Development, coaching or therapy, then it is extremely important that you are very sure that it is your own ideas, thoughts, behaviour patterns etc. that you start dealing with. If a belief or fixed trait is really others' opinions and ideas which you have taken on, it's a waste of time.

If you find something which is not your own, but something you have been persuaded to think, by others, or have borrowed from others, then it is actually possible to cut the connection to these things again. If Peter feels dominated by his father who says: "You are quite stupid", then that is the father's opinion, not Peter's. He must therefore CUT the connection to that opinion and realize that it is not his and "send it back to the father" right here and now.

Note carefully that he doesn't cut the connection to his father; that would violate the universal solvent of all problems: Communication!!

There could be a small danger here, namely if you disconnect from something that IS your own. Then you will never get it handled as you believe it isn't yours and have disconnected from it. Why handle other's stuff? But this very small danger is not difficult to get around as soon as you get a little practice in this.

Doubt, Want, Need, Deprivation and Limitation

These heavy challengers like to run a psycho-social meme on the rest of us, which is scarcity. There is a "lack". Money is "limited". There is "overpopulation". "Not enough to go round". "Someone has to be the loser".

This is completely at odds with the teachings of Buckminster Fuller (the US architect who invented geodesic domes), who said emphatically "We are all billionaires." The money just hasn't been shared around evenly. That was his platform.

Bucky was talking about limitless free energy that's out there. Yet they ration it, claim is it difficult to produce, and charge unconscionable amounts of money for something that belongs to all of us anyway. The universe is ours; all that's in it is ours; everybody's. Yet these creeps get protection from laws which say you and I can't have it. It's not everyone's; not the Creators (they say); it belongs to mega-corporations, which now act as if they own our planet (because they do).

They know of no lack or scarcity. They own it all. We get nothing, just a few crumbs at the feast table. It's no longer even possible to contain them with restricting laws, because they are above the law. No national laws apply to these massive multi-national conglomerations.

We are stuck with them. And it's part of this lack of freedom model: for them freedom is a quantity, not a quality as Per Schiøttz taught, and they are seeking to own and control it ALL.

OK, enough of the rant. Let's go back to psychology! Just remember there is this subtle sub-liminal reduction meme conditioning all our lives.

4. Procedure (For Self Or Clients)

First you must realise which persons, places or situations etc. you feel have caused you to make yourself smaller. For each of them in turn, you write down all the different ideas, thoughts, behaviour patterns, commands, unethical actions, opinions etc. etc., picked up from that person or place or in that situation.

You can explore these, using questions like:

What thought, attitude, command, idea, etc. came from [...] that you used to make yourself smaller?

Any dismissive or put-down gesture or facial expression of [...] that you used to make yourself smaller?

Did [...] give you any commands or advice that invalidated your own view?

Were there any religious, sexual, political, family or any other kind of enforced ideas or beliefs?

Then in your own universe you actually CUT the connection to these items, one at a time, realizing they are not yours and seeing whose they are at the same time. IT IS IMPORTANT TO MAKE YOUR SEVERANCE STATEMENT OUT LOUD.

If you come across something you have already disconnected from earlier, just acknowledge that. Finally you sign this "document" that you have actually disconnected from these things. The whole action can take some hours or weeks or months depending on the client's case load, but it is extremely important to do it very early on, for instance in a life quality coaching - if not as the very first action.

I, Peter Hansen, do herby cut the connection to my father's

    1. Invalidation by saying I am stupid
    2. Talking badly about me to my friends
    3. Attempts to decide:
        My education
        How to spend my money
        Whom I can date
        my haircut
        Which books I should read
        When to go to bed
    4. Lack of communication

Peter Hansen
Peter Hansen

Why?

When all this is done you ought to find out what has been missing in your written or unwritten ethical code, which caused you to allow your integrity to become less. Your own principles have left you vulnerable to being pipped. *Write down the missing self-protection principle as an addition to your ethical code.* If this is kept in times to come (eternal now's) it will act as a guarantee that you will never again allow your freedom to be lessened or taken away.

Here is an example of a handling Peter did regarding his father. It's a very ordinary example from a situation which is very common:

Addition to my ethical code:

It's my right to decide about my own life

Peter Hansen

Peter Hansen

When the revision to the code is completed and signed, you should experience more freedom and a growth as a person - again depending on the state of skills and awareness.

The most incredible results have occurred with this handling, including the "dominators" suddenly becoming friendly towards the pip. If there is no change or not a lot of growth, then there are still unhandled items or you have disconnected from something of your own that you should have kept.

The ability to "disconnect" can be very small in the beginning. Don't fret. It picks up pretty quickly and in the end the client will stay non-dominated with constant expanding freedom as the result.

Is this difficult?

If it turns out to be hard to deal with in this way, then another approach is needed first. What has happened is that the client has to a very large degree had his own personality mingled into others so it's almost impossible to find head nor tails in any of them. He can't see what is his and what's Daddy's. In this case, again depending on the case level, physical awareness (connectivity) processes, such as "Say hello to the physical world." [not described here: K S-M]

But in my experience, there are very darned few that do not respond to the handling described.

More freedom

If all this has been handled and everything not one's own is gone, and the feeling of more freedom is there, then it's time to look for things one wants to enhance which are one's own. But don't be surprised if you never see the client again. He might expand his freedom forever...

He or she doesn't need you any more!

Freedom to....

The new freedom should be used for doing new things, to be better at and to expand interest areas in life. "Free me from..." is only valid when it's not one's own stuff one wants to get rid of or be free from. Your own mental garbage heap is your own responsibility and you are the only one who can handle it.

Last step

I have used one more little action. In the above example I asked Peter to write down: "How is the real Peter...". This has almost always ended up in laughter galore and then tears of joy.

Note: I do not use a bio-feedback meter of any kind for these handlings. It complicates things and it's my opinion that if you can't get behind the client's facade and feel their emotional responses, using yourself for feed-back, then don't even try.

5. How Could So Many Be So Stupid?

Have you ever seen mass suppression? Many, many people being suppressed by the same one person or small group of persons or one thing? There are stellar examples of this in present society and in history too. I don't think there has been any time – on this planet – where there were not examples of mass suppression.

What is this phenomenon anyway? Let's take one of the stars: Adolph Hitler, "Der Führer". There is no question about his bad deeds, I am sure. If in doubt, consult history books, films and videos and go and see some of the World War II museums in Germany and France. You will know what I mean.

Where did Hitler get his power from? The people of course, you might say, and rightly so. Everybody admired him (at least in the beginning) for his fantastic (and fanatic) ideas of a free German people, only the people didn't live to see that freedom become theirs, as he stole the freedom from the people. They gladly gave their power to him by agreeing to his mad ideas and by adopting these crazinesses. This is how the people allowed themselves to be pipped by Herr Hitler.

If you can agree to the above explanation, then suppose everybody had turned their backs on Hitler. What power would he have then? Nothing! All the power he ever had was given to him by the people. Had they all, from Eva von Braun to the 14 year old private soldier in Hitler's army—all of them—turned their backs to him, he would have remained a snotty little corporal in a jail in Austria.

You can take any and every big bad terrible "Oppressor" in history, like Napoleon and Stalin, just to mention a couple more, and see that the pattern is exactly the same. Had everyone turned their backs on these cads, they would have had no power, nothing, zilch, nada. People would be free. These warlords have a strange idea that you can get peace by making war... how weird...

It is said—and I believe it—that Man is basically good. It doesn't say spiritual beings, it says Man, that means to me people on this planet. People being humanoid, members of the human race... Man (or even Humankind). And any folk on other planets too, and woman... (I do believe that it should encompass all beings too).

But some of these men and women act as though no one told them that they are good; good and decent deep down. To me it seems as though they think that freedom is a quantity not a quality, and they had better get whatever they can lay their dirty hands on. Then, when they do this, people around them make themselves smaller and get affected by these cads.

The cads CAN be helped. If you can get them into my coaching chair I know how to handle them - and it will be a pleasure for me to do so. They are good people, but they are stuck in an incident which they keep creating constantly in the Now. They think that the incident that was "then" is "now" and that the "now" is "then". Being in that mind-twisting incident looking at the future, forward from then, they get a terrible sight with death and destruction and no freedom, so they had better start grabbing.

All you have to handle is the actual mind-twisting incident, and they will be out of it instantly. That's the power of Supernoetics® piloting.

The source "creating" the existence and the conditions they see and create will be gone when they move to the present 'now'. We have the knowledge that's needed, and we can even start with ourselves actually - without breaking up relationships or families and without turning our backs on anyone or anything.

That's a very potent message of hope.

6. The Phenomenon Of Latent Gains

A very interesting aspect has appeared during the development of the Freedom Tools, of handling suppression with people who have had a lot of coaching, piloting or counseling therapy, whilst they were thoroughly pipped. By a "lot of coaching or therapy" I mean handling unwanted feelings, problems with communication, problems in general, upsets in life, problems in relationships, hidden destructive beliefs, problems at work and fixed ideas and stuck opinions etc.

It can be different from case to case but the common denominator is that the attempted self-encounters took place whilst there were several, even many, un-dealt with pipping situations on the case.

Of course, as pipping can be a heavily charged area, these people did not have big gains through their self-growth pathway, and very often they were pushed on to the next procedure or system, or found another guru, in the hope the difficulty could be resolved by other alternatives.

They were promised abilities that did not materialize, individually, or en masse, in their self-growth program. They had wins and insights, but these did not manifest themselves in real life. His or her life did not change after the counseling or coaching in the way it was promoted that it should.

Quite a few of them left their program or found another way of enhancement to follow, or even went into some false technique which did not address the pipping issue and thus did not take them anywhere either.

What is very amazing is that when they finally got the pipping off, all the earlier expected gains and changes in life started to show up, one by one. One case got his abilities gained from coaching on communication rehabilitated and his level of communication changed drastically without ever touching the issue of communication.

The same thing happened with another person who was dramatizing a lot of fixed ideas. After some handling of pipping, he completely stopped this and stopped making everybody around him wrong. His life took a new turn and he expanded his professional life into a totally new area for him. Amazing and wonderful to watch.

Another middle-aged professor, who was rather timid and insecure (even fearful) in his day-to-day life, suddenly announced with joy, "I have found courage!"

7. Freedom Is A Quality (Not A Quantity)

In the chapter "How To Gain More Freedom", I wrote: *The assumed dominator has misunderstood something. He thinks freedom is a quantity and therefore he has to keep others down in order to get the freedom for himself. Freedom is a quality – please!!*

Let us take a further look at this statement that Freedom is a *quality*!! But first some definitions, comments and examples to put us on the same page:

Be, Do and Have: One assumes a Beingness, from which actions are taken, resulting in something to have. This is the usual sequence and natural way things build up. Some people have this reversed, saying "If I HAVE, then I can DO and then I can BE (something)."

Example: If I have money, then I can travel and be famous and happy. If you inherit a bag of money, then you can travel – oh yes, and maybe you will be happy. When the money runs out your happiness will be gone. And if you don't know how to create or earn money, because you do not have the skills needed and because you are not a trained worker, then you can't get new money to spend in order to do things that make you happy and 'free'.

Money is a quantity, lots of money is a great quantity. You can say one million dollars, that's a quantity. You can say ten dollars, that is a smaller quantity. Quantities can be counted in different ways. Money can be counted in dollars or other currencies. Land can be measured in acres. Potatoes can be measured in kilograms, etc. etc. These countables are all physical things. These are things you can have. Usually you get things by earning a salary from doing a job, being a trained craftsman or similar. Be, Do, then Have is the right sequence.

If you have been trained to be a shipbuilder you can do shipbuilding and have ships and boats to sell and you can exchange the boats for money. The new money you earn can be used to expand your shipyard and build more or bigger boats, which will make you happier still, etc. etc. You reached your goal of expanding. This will give a feeling of joy and freedom. You will feel free to be, do and have. The state you have built up here by be, do and have is free, developing and enjoying it is free – that is freedom.

OK, again: be, do, have is the right sequence and can create joy and freedom.

Free from Be, Do and Have: Trying to get rid of something unwanted is of course not done from a happy state of mind. If you have an illness, something hurting or stopping you in some way, I am sure you are not the happiest person. And it gets worse if you can't get rid of the problem and get out of the situation. I am sure you will not feel free. At the very least, you are not getting rid of it. You are stuck in the unwanted condition.

If you get assigned a job you do not like to do you might protest or try to fake it or get rid of it; and in this situation you will not be happy or feel free either. If you are sick, or a failure, or a drop-out, you are not a happy person. There are things you will try to escape as you do not like to be that way. You might even think that freedom is getting rid of something, but it is not a happy state. This is reversed freedom, in some places called bondage or slavery.

Domination: There are two sides to this, the one being dominated and the other dominating. The dominating person is putting himself in front. He is the most important person in the world—or at least he is more important than the persons he dominates or tries to dominate. The person being dominated in a situation is usually overwhelmed or unsure of himself or his own abilities. He has very little self-esteem.

In order to keep the peace, he agrees with the dominating person (or factor). He might also be lower in the hierarchy he is part of and has the idea that *his* opinion counts less than the opinions of those higher in the hierarchy. Therefore he lets go of some of his values, opinions, positions, powers and self esteem and in this way he makes himself "smaller" and less able and less FREE. He experiences less FREEDOM.

When he makes himself smaller he goes down the scale. The scale of success, scale of empathy, scale of affinity, scale of understanding, scale of communication, scale of ability to do, be and have, scale of joy and scale of freedom.

When he hits the bottom of all scales he will be a battered and changed personality. He will have very little initiative left and needs orders when something has to be done. He might end up in a state where he will not do anything for fear of doing it wrong and being scolded and restricted and even fired or killed. He might end up being a very neurotic person (being the effect of some things) or even psychotic (being the effect of everything) depending on the severity of the domination and his own strength or lack of it.

The dominating person has fixed ideas, stuck opinions or crashing misunderstandings regarding freedom. A fixed idea or stuck opinion can very well be one he has subconsciously taken on during a traumatic incident where he lost. He was NOT the winner. He was in pain and suffered some kind of overwhelm. He got hurt in an accident, and later on he kept this traumatic incident under his awareness, under his consciousness and in this way he created or added to his own subconscious mind.

This hidden trauma might become activated later on by similarities in his present environment which might contain a person who is exhibiting great freedom, joy and ability to be, do and have. The person with the trauma sees this as threatening to himself because he might also have the mistaken idea that freedom is a quantity; and here is a guy who seems to have plenty, so "I better start grabbing". And he tries to dominate the other which makes him feel a weird kind of freedom, freedom from something unwanted that is. This twisted kind of 'freedom' is very often seen in people who take part in discussions, politics, religion, "freedom fights" and even war.

"Fighting for freedom", "Freedom fighters"; what a strange idea! Part of the package the dominating person is running is the inability to see differences, similarities and identical things. This inability gets projected onto the pip, who ends up thinking that some of the dominating person's characteristics are his own. If this goes on for any length of time, the two personalities can be so intertwined that neither of the persons can see head nor tail in this mess and start doubting their own personality and reality. It's very bad when they are unreal to themselves and lose sight of who they really are.

So: if all I have written here about domination is factual, i.e. something you can actually observe between people in their relationships, then there is a way to stop the effects of domination. Therefore I suggest that you observe the people in your environment and yourself in the relationships, and see if you can spot some domination. Because all it takes as per the above, is to get the pipped person to stop making himself smaller and getting the dominating person out of the trauma he is dramatizing.

This is what is described somewhat in the chapter "How To Gain More Freedom'. You can imagine how it will be for anyone to get rid of all those scary and awful things I wrote about above. I have seen it many, many times with my clients. It might take some time to get the dominating person out of the traumatic incident, and it might take some time to coach the pipped person through to a point where he can see what traits came from the other person that he adopted to make himself smaller.

But doing the program for real is very worthwhile – I promise you!

The Real Me

The easiest part to discover is the part where you have been dominated, not where you have dominated others. This is because being dominated gives you a bad feeling whereas dominating others gives you a better feeling—even though it is false. Therefore, in coaching, the most time is used to work with domination received (pipping).

When all the pipping situations and all the dominating persons have been discovered and defused, clients obtain a sincere and joyful feeling of freedom. At this point they have got rid of all the ideas, commands, attitudes, self-limiting beliefs, etc. etc. which came from the dominator, so they again can see who they really are.

The last step I do with them on the handling is to have them take and sheet of paper and write down: The real Joe is....: and then all the qualities they have... and it is amazing when they look at their own list. You will hear the most interesting statements like: "I knew this" or "I never knew this". Of course, big surprise. Usually tears flow at this point and that's when the hugs start being handed around!

Note: The dominating person does NOT have to be a bad person. It is easy to see him as bad because having been connected to him you have made yourself smaller and therefore see the connection as bad - as well as any subject connected to it. The dominating person might not be a dominating person for everybody around him, because the domination in fact is granted by the dominated person as it is HIM who makes HIMSELF smaller. And therefore, in the final analysis, it is him who ultimately is the responsible person. The dominating person might, in turn, also feel dominated himself by others, in the manner of the famous little poem by mathematician Augustus de Morgan:

Big fleas have little fleas upon their backs to bite 'em,

And little fleas have lesser fleas, and so, *ad infinitum*.

And the great fleas, themselves, in turn, have greater fleas to go on;

While these again have greater still, and greater still, and so on.

8. Personality Confusion

In the section "Is this difficult?" in the chapter "How to gain more freedom" I wrote:

"If it turns out to be hard to handle this way, then another approach is needed first. What has happened is that the client has, to a very large degree, got his own personality mingled into others so it's almost impossible to find head nor tail in any of this. He can't see what is his and what's Daddy's."

After years of domination from Daddy, Peter can't really see what his own opinions are, and which ones in fact came from Daddy. That is, what beliefs are originally Daddy's that Peter has taken on and actually *made* his own. In this way Peter has added something to his own belief system. As he has lived with that for many years it has actually become part of his own personality, part of his way of being and doing and having, resulting in the way he has things and the things he has collected or not been able to have.

If you want to ask Peter to reject something which was Daddy's originally, Peter will not be able to do this as he will not be able to see the difference between himself and Daddy, at least not in some of the personality traits or ways of living.

Peter's way of being, doing and having is exactly like Daddy's on some points and Peter will not be able to see what originally was Daddy's and what is his own. Therefore, when he does not see any difference he will have a very hard time to put a distance between the two viewpoints and eventually also to separate himself out from what originally came as a command, order, thought or idea from Daddy. Because Peter made it his own! Adding something from another in this way made him smaller.

An example could be Daddy's opinion about haircut. Daddy is from an earlier generation when a haircut was supposed to be short back and sides. In Peter's generation it has suddenly become the fashion to have long hair. Peter wants to follow this fashion too, in order to be fully accepted by his mates. Daddy forbids this and Peter gets another short haircut. This idea is adopted by Peter and he has short hair for the rest of his life. He has come to dislike men and boys with longish hair and he might even impose the opinion about haircuts on his own sons. They might not like to be told how to cut their hair, so they might protest –and upsets appear every time their hair is a bit too long for Peter's taste. Peter's opinion about haircuts, he thinks, is now his own and he fights for it, even though actually it originally was his father's.

In order to create more freedom for Peter it is necessary to get his and Daddy's ideas separated out a bit before Peter can see what is his own and what is his father's. First, he has to see them as ideas stemming from his father and then decide if they should be his ideas too - or if he should disconnect from them.

For this purpose I have developed a question sheet to handle this problem, called the Personality De-Mix. There are 9 sets of questions. Always start with the first set:

- Tell me a similarity between _____ and you !
- Tell me a difference between _____ and you !

You of course, put the name of the person in question where the blank line is. In this case you would write in "Daddy" or "Your father".

Choose the wording that works best for Peter. Then you ask the two questions alternately like a, b, a, b, a, etc.

When this has gone to a flat point or no more answers you do the question set 2, etc. in the same way, in the most applicable sequence.

If you know that the mix-up of Peter's and Daddy's characteristics has caused strange things that Peter has, then you can do question 4 as the next option.

You only do the Two Way Discussion in 9 if you have not yet reached an effective result, which should be some kind of personality shift or statement to the effect that Peter now sees better what is his or Daddy's.

Peter might state that he feels more free and more himself. Watch out for these kind of statements which indicates that the process has done what it was supposed to do and you should end off here with a good acknowledgement of what Peter saw. Don't go on too long. It might go very fast, and in some cases it will go flat with some good realisation already after questions 1a and 1b.

Be alert!

Personality De-Mix

1.   a. Tell me a similarity between _____ and you?

        b. Tell me a difference between _____ and you?

2.   a. What is _____ that you are also?

        b. What is _____ that you are not?

c. What is _____ not, that you are also not?

d. What is _____ not, that you are?

3.   a. What does _____ do, that you also do?

b. What does _____ do, that you don't do?

c. What does _____ not do, that you don't do either?

d. What does _____ not do, which you do?

4.   a. What does _____ have, which you also have?

b. What does _____ have which you do not have?

c. What does _____ not have, which you don't have either?

d. What does _____ not have, which you have?

5.   a. What does _____ know, that you also know?

b. What does _____ know, that you don't know?

c. What does _____ not know, that you don't know either?

d. What does _____ not know, that you know?

6.   a. Which weakness has _____ that you also have?

      b. Which weakness has _____ that you don't have?

      c. Which strength has _____ that you also have?

      d. Which strength has _____ that you don't have?

7.   a. Which responsibility has _____ that you also have?

      b. Which responsibility has _____ that you don't have?

      c. Which responsibility does _____ not have, that you also
         don't have?

      d. Which responsibility does _____ not have, that you
         have?

8.   a. Who is _____ being which you are also being?

      b. Who is _____ being which you are not being

9.   2-way discussion: In what way do you think that _____
      will influence your life, in the future?

9. Freedom Tools – Addition 1:

As more and more people study the Freedom Tools, more and more viewpoints read the materials and during studying their essays, which they write as part of the course, it becomes apparent to me that there are things in the text, that can be written in a clearer way. These extra writings will appear as additions until enough have accumulated, so that a whole new issue of Freedom Tools will be called for and produced.

This is the first addition:

Procedure (For Self And Clients): (section 5)

Don't try to cut the connection to those things that came from his father (which he used to make himself smaller) in one go. I didn't make myself clear. It works best if these items are handled one by one as follows:

Coach: do the first one!

Peter: I Peter Hansen, do hereby cut the connection to my father's *invalidation by saying I am stupid*, as I realise that this is HIS and not my characteristic. (Disconnects).

Coach: Good, have you disconnected from that?

Peter: Yes.

Coach: Good, next one!

Peter: I Peter Hansen, do hereby cut the connection to my father's *talking badly about me to my friends*, as I realise that this is HIS and not my characteristic. (Disconnects). Yes I have done that!

Coach: Good, next one...

Peter: I Peter Hansen... etc. etc..

When Peter has disconnected to all the items on the list, then and only then, he then signs this document and keeps it.

Doing it this way is more specific and works better than doing all items as one big generality.

Per Schiøttz

October 9th 2018

10. Freedom Tools
Expanded Procedure

[Per expanded the procedure with the following steps, which he sent to me only a matter of days before he died: K S-M].

Step 1. Finding a target:

Find which persons or groups your client has had trouble with, and consequently made self smaller.

This could also be a situation, but persons or groups can usually be picked out of situations.

These items can be found by looking through earlier notes or records made regarding the client. They can also be found by interview.

Here are some interview questions that can be used. Some will cover big areas and when the area has been located you will have to sort it out and find the persons/groups you are looking for, namely those who caused your client make him or her self smaller:

"Are there persons or groups, in relationships with whom, you made yourself smaller?"

"Are there situations where you had a hard time 'standing your ground'?" (Towards who?)

"Do you feel being effect of something from a past life?" (What, when, who?)

"Are you being haunted?" (By who?)

"Has someone cast a spell on you?" (Who?)

"Are there any problems in your area?"

"Are there any problems at your work?"

"Are there any problems with relatives?"

"Did you ever feel you were:
1. *dominated*
2. *suppressed*
3. *overwhelmed*
4. *made wrong*
5. *unmocked*
6. *threatened*
7. *forced*
8. *inhibited*
9. *invalidated*
10. *Robbed of something*
11. *Forced to accept something*
12. *Denied having something*
13. *Told to BE in a certain way*
14. *Told not to BE in a certain way*
15. *Told to do something you didn't want to do*
16. *Told not to do something you wanted to do*
17. *Threatened with consequences*
18. *Traumatized*

These are only examples. The list can be extended indefinitely. You can add questions *ad libitum* and form new ones applicable to where you know your client lives. Expect to find many, but don't continue looking for them when you find a hot item; then it's time to handle the hot item, and when completely done, you can revert to these questions and find new hot items.

Each client has many, many items. Handling a few will make him feel better. Handling many will make him feel much better. Handling all the charged ones, will change his life and he will never, ever make himself smaller again.

Step 2. Handling The Item:

Let's say that you have found the item Joe. Now you need to brief your client on the procedure and what is expected of him/her. Best scenario is where client has already studied the Pips and Pipping book. This is the very best approach. Next best is having client read the section: "How to gain more freedom?" If you are already in session with the client and he/she hasn't read any of the Freedom Tools materials, then you can brief him as much as needed with the following procedure:

We are going to find what happened in your (kind of relationship) to Joe, i.e. what came from Joe which you in any way, shape or form used to make yourself smaller.

Examples:

It could be something Joe said, meaning the words, like: "I think you are crazy", "Do you really believe that?", "I don't believe that", "That is wrong", "You are too old for that", "You are too young for that", "That is for girls/women", "That is for boys/men", "Are you really religious?", "That is for kids", etc.

It could be the way Joe spoke, like: With anger, in disgust, with disbelief, sneakingly, cunningly, convincingly, sadly, with a big laugh, apathetically, with "poisonous" voice, with demonstrative cough, etc.

It could be Joe's body language, like: frowning, rolling eyes up/down, shrugging, slowly shaking his head, making faces, waving you off, pointing your way out, kicking you, slapping you, punching, pushing, turning his back to you, etc. are all obvious ways of putting someone down.

It may just be an intention to order you to do something (his command); make you do it his way; make you behave differently; cause you to misown something; have you own up to something not yours or not your doing (I know you did it...); make you look like you know less; or sneeringly put you down with supposed flattering words, like: "You are SO clever", etc.

You may already know the phrase "To damn with faint praise", meaning, yes, you are saying something complementary but being so understated it amounts to a put down.

It can be more subtle: Joe's actions, like speaking "behind your back", talking bad about you to others (who you heard it from), cutting the communication (slamming down the phone), forcing you physically, impersonating being you, using your name/signature, not keeping appointments, stealing from you, interrupting, scolding, talking down, not giving back something borrowed from you, etc.

Ideas, voiced or not, like: writing you orders that are difficult or impossible to follow (so you make a fool of yourself), telling you what to think/do, trying to persuade you in religious, political, military, sporting, hobby, musical, art, sexual games, relational, family, or social matters and other beliefs, etc. so that you set aside your own viewpoint.

If this seems to be a lot of different areas to look into, then you are right, because we are talking about an entire life and all that could have happened in it. Main point here is for client to see that there is nothing that is not valid, because nobody can tell beforehand, what will make us make ourselves smaller.

What is found is, one at a time, put on a list as part of a broader statement, which is written across the top of the paper, followed by the items, one after another.

"I (...name...), do hereby cut the connection to Joe's (item, item, item) as I realize that these are his and not mine."

Then list the items, one by one.

When the list is complete, which means that your client has completely exhausted all the things that came from Joe which he used to make self smaller, THEN it is time to do the disconnections. Joe's paper now looks like Peter Hansen's in the materials under Procedure, only it hasn't been signed by your client yet.

Disconnection: Have your client sit back comfortably, paper in hands and disconnect from all the items one by one. This is done in client's own universe and is basically a statement about not anymore making self smaller because of these items, one by one. See the examples in Freedom Tools – addition 1.

It is a decision that the item is Joe's and does not have to be owned by your client too. If needed, to make this more real, you can ask client to please send this item back to Joe with a "Thanks for lending!" You will find how your particular client does this best.

Make sure that each disconnection has actually taken place. The client should go brighter and brighter as he get's through the disconnections. If he gets to the end and nothing happened, he even looks worse, then something has been missed and you need to find the missing items as in Step 2.

Go back and find them and have the list extended. If he says there are no more, ask him if you have passed a good point doing this (something occurred and you missed it, or he didn't mention it, pending his openness and case shape). If still no go, ask him how he is doing and what he thinks of these disconnections, watch for a good point or hidden good result that he/she isn't voicing.

If still no go, write down your observations and get advice from your supervisor.

If, as is usually the case, he looks brighter, happier and might have voiced some realization(s), then ask him if he would like to sign this document, and let him do so. Tell him to keep his document (disconnection statement) and look at it from time to time, as needed, and in case something else comes up, add it, and do the disconnection himself again.

Step 3. Ethical Code Addition:

Take a look in the materials at the section called "Ethics and Philosophy". Doing this step is with the intention that client will never again connect up to things like he has just disconnected from. Otherwise, if he just walks out and does it again, we have wasted our and his time.

So his addition to his ethical code has to be real, has to be something he can keep, not just something which is valid in high spirits. Especially when things get rough. Coach him to look at his addition to his ethical code and describe HOW it will prevent him to connect up with those things he has just disconnected from – even if the going get's tough!

The client is usually in high spirits after just having completed Step 2, he sees clearer here, what to include in his ethical code. If he has added something which seems a "step too far", then you can take a look at it in a later session in order to reword it to make it real and doable. You always do Step 3 after having done a Step 2. The disconnections regarding the next item might demand a new addition to the ethical code - don't forget!

Step 4. Finding/Handling The Next Item:

This is one item down – very good. Give the client a break a couple of days if he had a good win. If not schedule the next session very soon, like tomorrow if possible. You have to play this by ear, based on your knowledge of the client. The rule is that the heavier charged the case is, the more you go for short flights or sessions. This is because he might have less energy as long as he is highly charged up, and will have a harder time to concentrate for longer periods. You short-session him. End *on the first win* every session, either for a shorter or longer break. This is more important than to complete items or steps.

Now you go to the next item, this means the next hot item you found with Step 1, and take that through Step 2. If you did not get more items in Step 1, then you go back and continue with Step 1, until you find the next hot item and take that through Step 2. If you at any point have a hard time to evaluate how hot an item is, like "Should we do this one or not" then ask the client if he would be interested in doing it. Going by clients interest is a kind of guarantee that you will not push him out intro something he/she can't handle.

After Step 2 you do Step 3 again as described above. Then next item, etc. Until all areas of life have been covered and all questions in Step 1 have been exhausted and both you and client are sure that there is nothing more to handle on this rundown with this technique. If your client hasn't changed his life to something much better, then you should expand on Step 1 again.

Step 5. This Is The Real Me:

This Step 5 isn't necessarily done fifth! Meaning that it could be applicable after any big breakthrough, with the client in a state of Zen-like cheerfulness and calm.

This is up to coach's evaluation. It is a wonderful step but doesn't really call for being done more than once. This step validates and acknowledges the client for the person he really is without any trauma, disabilities, making self smaller, feeling pipped or suppressed - when he is really himself.

I often ask clients to give me a copy of this statement or I note it down myself in my notes as we go, and then after the session I print it up as big as I can on A3 size paper if possible in smart letters and give it to client (or mail it) and ask him to put it up over his bed or somewhere where he will see it daily and never forget or lose sight of who he really is.

[I usually tell the client to write themselves a recurring message on their cell phone, to display daily for at least a few weeks, until the new belief becomes natural. Per liked this suggestion but admitted he would not have thought of it. He was not a geek or "cellphone person", being already 79 when he died. Keith Scott-Mumby]

This step almost always ends up in lots of happiness, hugging and tears of joy.

End Result:

It has been remarked above that the ultimate "end result" is that the hostile or domineering person whose behavior has pipped our client (that is, caused him or her to pip self!) will suddenly have a change of heart. He or she, without being prompted, will suddenly try to communicate in a friendly way. It may be direct: he or she phones the client. It may be indirect, as a message via a mutual acquaintance.

Just one way or another, the oppressor originates the contact. We don't prime the client with this knowledge. Just wait till he or she reports something of the kind as a natural course of conversation.

It is impossible to say where in this desirable end result will occur (it can also occur many times, actually). You know, that the person who was "dominating" turned to the "dominated" in a new and friendly fashion. But this is a technical result. The proof that the process did what it was supposed to do. It may not be an instant change in demeanor. *But it will occur sooner or later.* How much it means to the client is very different in each case. Some get into total awe or amazement and you won't be able to touch them for a long time, some will take it as a natural thing item to item and actually expect it to happen every time.

Above all, have fun!!

Per Schiøttz

Copenhagen, October 24th 2018

Message From Beyond The Grave

Dear Friend,

I hope that you understand these materials. I have worked with them and this case aspect of clients' cases since 1989 and have gained quite a lot of experience with this. I find the handling of this case aspect extremely important, in order for the rest of the coaching to go smoothly.

I can observe this in individuals where this case aspect has been handled move a lot faster than cases who did not get this case aspect handled in the very beginning of their coaching history. This is because, if it is NOT handled and your client has the smallest misconceptions or misownership of some case aspects he might be wasting time working on something which in fact is not his. Then he had better 'send it back' to the rightful owner and start on his own garbage heap, so to speak.

Seeing a case aspect in another, from the other's viewpoint, is possible, but it is a lot easier to handle one's own stuff, and then let the other handle his/her stuff because he/she is the best person to do so. When that is done you can enjoy another's viewpoint to the fullest extent and understanding.

If you would like to use these materials with your clients you are very welcome to do a free extension course which will teach you to use the materials in the way I have found they work the best.

But, do not forget to have fun too. If it is not fun, all the way, there might be something wrong and we need to have a talk!

Per Schiøttz

[It takes 3 days full time and one week part-time as an estimated average. You will be working with someone directly online, using SKYPE or Zoom, which Per stipulated would be free of charge]

APPENDIX 1

These two appendices were not written by Per Schiøttz, which is why they are appended to the main booklet.

Social and Cultural Pipping

By Keith Scott-Mumby MD, MB ChB, PhD

Not mentioned by Per but social and cultural traps and discord can create pipping situations for the sensitive or at-risk individual. I felt I should write this additional section...

A young Asian friend of ours, a wealthy and successful realtor (a millionairess at twenty six), is under constant pressure from her parents to move back into the "proper" family home. She doesn't want to go back, having found her freedom.

This vibrant youngster recognizes all the cultural stigmas and taboos of her ethnic background. Living at home, as a woman, she'll be told what to do, where to work, who to marry, when to take a vacation, what to do with her money (which becomes family money) and so on. Having made all her own decisions for many years and become extremely successful, she has no intention of taking this regressive step.

But make no mistake, her parents want her back under their thumb, to bully, coerce and control. They want her pipped. Only her refusal to make herself smaller and give in to her parents stops her from becoming overwhelmed by "cultural pipping".

Arranged Marriages

This is another hot area. Certain cultures take it as a given that marriages will be arranged by parents from both sides. To live under such a burden of control, the young people must subdue their own desires and give in to what cynical and often heartless adults think is a right and proper match.

Love has no place in this schema and falling in love with someone of your own choice will only lead to heartache or, in certain cultures, violence. Many young Pakistani women have ended up in bloody pieces, stuffed in bin liners, and scattered all over the city, because they tried to runaway from this system.

Ironically, the system is held in place by the older women, not by men, as you would think. Their attitude seems to be: "I had to do as I was ordered and make a loveless match. Why should you be able to as you wish? You will marry who you are told to marry." Since they were forced into a relationship by their parents, instead of taking pity on their offspring as you might expect, these women want to perpetuate the suffering inherent in the system.

Snobbery

This too is a kind of pipping. The English social "class system" was built on a pecking order (or perhaps one should say pipping order) of status. All too often, those at the top are haughty and dismissive of the "lower orders" (an actual term in frequent use).

I was raised in the shadow of this system. My mother, a cleaner, skivvy and sometime seamstress, absolutely knew her place in this class hierarchy and brought my up to overvalue those higher on the ladder. It meant I was pipped and made to feel small, unimportant and even slightly stupid. The rich elite have always fostered the view that poor folk are either lazy or dumb. It suits them to think so.

As I child, it's arguable whether I could be said to have pipped myself or made myself smaller. I just grew up with certain rules of status and value. But pipped I was. Only when I finally went to college did I shrug off these rules of social order. Millions of us did, as the 1960s got under way and we wanted to be free and express ourselves. We simply rebelled.

I have always celebrated the 60s as the most important decade in the entire history of Humankind. There was such a thrust towards personal freedom that has never been manifest, before or since. We thought we would change the world for ever, as in a way we did. But the drug culture and its special version of pipping and slavery soon brought this golden age of freedom to an end.

Ex-Pats

Vivien pointed out that ex-pat communities abroad, to this day, are notoriously snobby. Europeans have always looked down on the locals, who were made to feel lowly and inferior, simply because of race, religion or color.

Ex-pats seem to stick to their own circle and don't want to mix socially with "natives" and inter-racial love affairs, or (God forbid!) mixed-race marriages to a local, were looked upon with a species of horror that is hard to understand in today's world.

Of course this superiority attitude persists in today's racism and inter-religious wars. I would not like to be raised a black man in the USA, for example. Armed or unarmed, victims of color are killed by police at approximately twice the rate of white Caucasians.

These comments are not meant to point out that ex-pats and other racists are, or can be, nasty people. The real point is that there is considerable pressure on certain social and cultural groups to adopt the position of making themselves smaller; in other words, becoming pips.

It might be life saving to shut up and subdue yourself.

I have always delighted in the exact opposite from my dear wife Vivien! She hates ex-pat communities and their snooty attitudes, as surely as she loves mixing with the natives. On our honeymoon in Sri Lanka, I suddenly realized I'd "lost" her. An hour later a got a phone call: she'd gone home with the taxi driver, to meet with his family. When I found her, she was sitting in a shack by the ocean, with a giggling mob of kids at her knee, drinking the local brew (tea). They were very honored and moved by her informality. A far cry from the days of British rule (Ceylon).

Cults

Cults are another problem. There are many definitions of a so-called cult. The important point is that, in a cult, the individual submerges his or her own viewpoint to that of the tribe. There are always rules and these are concentrated on taking away the individual's freedom (often dressed up as "finding freedom") and imposing the equivalent of marshal law.

The Scientology headquarters of today have pseudo-police, swaggering about with guns and handcuffs, to keep the faithful in line and to prevent escape.

Individuals are forced to disconnect from their natural family and subjugated to the Empire. This is a line taken by all cults, from Scientologists and Jihadists, to the Jesus Army: "Your own folks are not welcome. They are bad people. Keep away from them. You'll be corrupted."

Sometimes there are punishments, which can be very harsh, to train a person to conform and surrender their sovereignty of mind to the cult leader. Those who rise to such positions of power are, by definition, dominators and controllers. Most often they are shriveled, inadequate personalities, who like to grab as much freedom as they can for themselves; freedom always stolen from cult members.

Online Bullying and Pipping

Bullying at school is a major problem in all the world's countries. It amounts to children pipping others, often with impunity, and causing them to grow up broken or hurting, before they even really get started. I might even remark that teachers, as well as fellow pupils, will often resort to bullying hapless or weak children. It's disgraceful but it happens.

Today, moreover, we have cyber-bullying: dysfunctional or warped youngsters using texting and social media to humiliate, bully and insult their class mates. For reasons I'll leave others to explain, this seems to be more a phenomenon of brooding, hormonal young females trying to abuse and hurt weaker classmates, though of course males do it too, to some degree.

Then there is online trolling. It's easy to get tripped up and become a pip with this phenomenon. When it strikes it can truly wreck a person's life, work, relationships and peace of mind.

What is an online troll? Trolls take their name from the fairy-story characters who prowl the woodlands, byways and bridges, looking for people to eat up and destroy. While fairy-story trolls are only fictional characters, there are some real-life trolls that behave just like them. In fact, these real-life trolls live in the shadows of cyberspace with the sole purpose of leaping out and making people's lives miserable.

In general, trolls are people who intentionally attack others online by posting offensive comments, despicable lies, or damaging pictures (which may be Photoshopped even). When a person is attacked online for their beliefs, thoughts, work, opinions or physical appearance, this is called trolling.

This is not quite the same as online bullying, when the target is typically one exact person. The troll doesn't care who they hit, so long as trouble is stirred up and he or she gets a reaction. Don't respond! Just delete the remark or comment and hope they go away. Never respond. That's what the troll is hoping for.

And don't get pipped. Don't shrink. The person doesn't know you, so how could they be making an accurate judgment? "Not logical," as Mr. Spock used to say (Star Trek 1).

It's important to rid yourself of the pain of those times and upgrade your view of self. Supernoetics® piloting happens to be about the best way to do this.

Self-Pipping

Finally, at this point, I should throw in some remarks about a person pipping him or herself, for no particular reason (that is, no outside agency). Doing yourself down is something we have all been guilty of, at some time or another.

For this I am reminded of an old adage (15th century) that really works: *comparisons are odious*. It means you can come to bad conclusions by comparing things that are not alike. It's a habit you should drop. Comparing yourself to other people will often mean to judge yourself to be inferior; there are always people with more money, faster cars, better looking dates or perhaps better grades in class.

Why beat yourself up by saying "I'm not as good as this or that person"? Trust me, if you stop doing that, the world will seem a safer, friendlier place. Beware the TV ads that try to make you envious of others, so you are induced to buy something that will make you more like them, so they tell you. They show pictures of wildly happy people (actors, pretending, remember) and the plan is that you sigh and say to yourself: "I want what they have got." So you go and buy one...

It's a continuous diet of inferiority: you are nobody without this dress-watch-car-gizmo-smartphone extra. It leads to bad self-pipping.

There are endless ways to pip one's self. I stole a library book once, as a teen; I still have it. But it nagged at me for decades, before I finally made up my mind to donate $100 anonymously to the library in question. Not that the missing book would be much of a loss to others; it was a translation of an old Norse saga "Egil's Saga". It had only ever been checked out twice, in the previous twenty years!

But I still felt like a rat and told myself I was a bad person. That's pipping!

On another occasion, once again in my teens, I was paralyzed for words when a pretty girl asked me to her home. She played some popular records of the day but I was absolutely tongue-tied and could not speak a single word to her. It was horrifying. You may be sure that, as I fled to safety, I made myself very small indeed.

That was then, this is now, as they say. No-one who knows me today could imagine me being overcome by shyness!

Thing is, we often don't give ourselves the breaks we would accord others. People like me have always given themselves a bad time; been very intolerant of our own mistakes or personal failures; painted the picture of smallness and worthlessness; something we wouldn't typically do to others.

All you have ever read of the "inner critic" in popular psychology—that nagging self-destructive voice within—could be redefined as the phenomenon of making one's self smaller; self-pipping if you like (I don't use that term).

Hacking The "Inner Critic"

A great restorative exercize for anyone, that does not need a coach or therapist to be present, is to take a number of sheets of paper and put down as many of these moments as you can recall, times when you alone made yourself smaller, for your own internal reasons. Really work to grow the list. You'll find scores, if not hundreds, of times when you hurt yourself, without anyone else being there to help you do it!

Then follow Per's procedure given in these pages: disconnect from each moment, one by one, by saying OUT LOUD: *I hereby repudiate the ridiculous act of making myself smaller. I restore myself to full life, joy and confidence. I forgive myself for my earlier folly. I no longer carry this moment with me, except as a lesson. I am learning to be the real me, in full freedom!*

Then don't forget to write a new description of "the REAL me" and create a new rule for your Ethical Codex. Never let it happen again. Cherish, admire and support yourself, at all times, on all occasions, in any circumstances (your own wording, of course).

Now remember, doing this you are lowering your stress levels, starting to bombproof your emotions, reducing cortisol levels, improving heart rate variability and getting to a better place, in mind AND body. Trauma is stored; that's a fundamental truth in Supernoetics®.

So let it out! You'll be glad you did.

APPENDIX 2

By Keith Scott-Mumby MD, MB ChB, PhD

I include this 2015 essay as a wider context for the topic of pipping and also to relate it to a number of conventional labels for disturbed individuals. Per read and admired the piece, though we never got chance before he died to discuss whether it would make a suitable addition to his materials.

Consequently, this is my own submission.

It is part of a long series of related essays, which I have called my "Natural Justice" series.

Social Order and Congruity

Justice, ethics and morals are very tricky subjects. These have screwed up many worthy human enterprises. Ancient Rome was once great and mighty; but by the time it got to killing people for amusement in the amphitheaters and nailing people to crosses to decorate the roadsides, it was all over, bar the Vandals and Goths.

It's about good behavior.

Religious groups, which ought to be teaching people autonomous self-control, nevertheless seek to dominate the individual with rules of conduct. Rarely indeed are these man-made "laws" wise or helpful but if you are a curious observer you will notice there is always at least one rule about obeying the priest classes, or risk being damned by hellfire for eternity! These power "laws" are usually enforced with ostracism, expulsion, violence or even death.

Indeed, the infamous Catholic Church thought nothing of burning to death those who stepped out of line. Better a dead rebel than a living threat to authority seems to have been their motto. Burning, beheading, stoning to death, skinning alive, slow roasting and the death of a thousand cuts are among the many devilish torments invented by those who want to maintain their power.

Today Islam seems the apotheosis of violence and barbarity. It's hard not to see a streak of sadism and cruelty in this current obsession with stonings, hangings, shootings and beheadings. The thing is, this murderous rampage may not be what mainstream Islam is all about but rather it is a power-crazed frenzy, driven by wily old washed-out authoritarian has-beens (the belligerent mullahs). They haven't any balls left—but they do have a nasty attitude and want to vent it by thrusting testosterone-crazy youth, in its prime, into the breach for the pursuit of their self-serving sexual and depraved fantasies, which they disguise as religious doctrine.

Communism isn't exactly a religion but it also takes its place as the origin of mass slaughter, probably the worst offender in this respect. According to Harold Eberle in his book *Christianity Unshackled: Are You A Truth Seeker?* (Destiny Image Publishers, 2009), Stalin was responsible for about 20 million deaths and Mao Tse Tung's regime for approximately 70 million.

Pohl Pot, who led the Communist Party faction known as the Khmer Rouge, killed over 1.5 million of his own Cambodian people. Add to these numbers the atrocities committed by Soviet dictators like Lenin, Khrushchev, and Brezhnev.

Throw in Fidel Castro and Kim Jong-il and, in total, Marxist regimes have slaughtered more than 100 million people within the last century. It all makes Hitler seem like a boy scout. Yet we had no hesitation wiping him off the face of the Earth.

Today, the Marxists are lining up to get the slaughter re-started. I see from the news that Greece has been foolish enough to vote itself a death government (sorry, a left-wing regime). I was grimly amused, actually: what was their *very first* thought after being elected? Get the house in order? Solve the economic worries? Get our own people back to work?

Nah, it was *let's grab the rest of Europe and make them communist too!* Marxism never succeeded at anything, yet its murderous proponents have never hesitated to force it on others. They can't make it work at home but that doesn't stop them inflicting their ideology on every nation they can coerce.

Morals

Morals is a much overused word and basically means someone else telling you how to live your life: invariably a wizened old mean-spirited crank with a poor attitude about life, love, happiness, creativity, sexuality and all the other God-given joys we may experience (a priest figure, in other words).

Ethics today is mainly a posh word for the same thing. Ethics is the subject of wrangling and argument in academic departments, which have little or no connection with the real world and no understanding of what it is based on. They dispute over what is the "right" thing to do, with no actual context and relation to the problems you and I really face. Hence ethics is seen as sterile and meaningless.

These same halls of academia have latterly become obsessed with game theory; working out who wins at what and how, as if that were the ultimate arbiter of what is a "successful" action and what is not. See, for example, the "prisoner's dilemma" game. It is supposed to help understand what governs the balance between cooperation and competition in business, in politics, and in social settings.

In the traditional version of the game, the police have arrested two suspects and are interrogating them in separate rooms. Each can either confess, thereby implicating the other, or keep silent. No matter what the other suspect does, each can improve his own position by confessing. If the other confesses, then one had better do the same to avoid the especially harsh sentence that awaits the one who holds out. If the other keeps silent, then one can obtain the favorable treatment accorded a state's witness by confessing.

Thus, confession is the dominant strategy for each. But when both confess, the outcome is worse for both than when both keep silent. What to do for the best? Can "prisoners" extricate themselves from the dilemma and sustain cooperation when each has a powerful incentive to cheat? If so, how?

Gradually, through time, these game theories have become eroded down to what is a "right" action is one that wins the game. This is very limited. The action we aspire to in Supernoetics® is winning the "total game" (long-range freedom, creativity and power), not some theoretical or artificial tricky situation.

Validity Of Action

Better than terms like "morals" and even "ethics", is our expression *congruity*. There's a whole Natural Justice piece on that. It is, in essence, validity on the 12 Channels Of Being. By bringing in all 12 Channels, we raise the game to the highest possible level and there are no variant options: winning is then a valid choice. I am talking about attaining limitless Being and infinite grace.

The important point I make is that right and wrong, good and bad, moral or wicked, ethical or nonsense, all really boils down to one central precept: rationality (reason). It's another way of looking at sanity. What makes sense?

Congruity is simply saying what you think and doing what you say. Per Schiøttz always insisted to me that true congruity is doing what you know you should do and not doing what you know you should not do. Simple really.

An action is congruent (good/moral/valuable) to the degree it sustains the highest spiritual values and the maximum positive gain for the most Channels (in other words, Jeremy Bentham's *Utilitarianism*). It becomes the action or choice that makes most sense, in the most spheres, in the maximum areas of responsibility. To figure out what that step or choice is requires sound reasoning. Madness or UN-sanity (Korzibski's term) runs counter to that reason.

So I repeat my teaching: good, proper, moral, right, ethical, sound and survivalist all add up to the same things: rationality, reason, intelligence, long-term gratification, continuity, common sense, sanity! *That's* congruity.

It goes without saying you cannot possibly be congruent and rationalize fully, without full knowledge of the 12 Channels Of Being. If you are not familiar with this magnificent thought-structure, you should learn about it. Go to www.supernoetics.com and use the search function to find it.

The Cheats In Life

Our own game of working for the purposeful reinvention of mankind®
is made difficult by encountering very degraded and confused beings,
who cannot seem to see past their own immediate gratification, into
higher realms of Being. They are, if you like, "cheats" at the game of
life.

At least, intentionally or unintentionally, they consistently come up
with adverse answers which affect the rest of us and make matters
difficult. The game where everyone wins, for example, can become
corrupted by such individuals, to the point where somebody has to get
hurt, for the sake of the common good.

The rise in Nazism is a case in point; not so difficult to decide what to
do. This evil regime had to be stopped at all costs, before the "1,000
years of darkness" predicted by Winston Churchill could descend
upon Humankind. But taking action cost a great many lives. Yes, it's
true, an early bullet through Hitler's head could hardly have been con-
sidered murder.

But what about the mad profit-driven rush to start cloning human
bodies? Who can foresee what lies ahead? Yet the rush to get there is
dragging us all into a situation that may require a great deal of pain,
setbacks and even death to extricate ourselves.

Adverse Personality Types

Adverse (definition): contrary, counter to the common good, in reverse direction, set against, opposed to; literally "turned against",
from the Latin. Also appears as the word *adversary*; opponent.

Let me introduce a few adverse personality types that Supernoetics®
wizards need to be aware of and steer around. These individuals are
running counter to the common good and if you are not wary, they
could bring you down, or an organization.

These are given various names but labeling is mere detail. There is
little difference, for example, between a narcissist and a psychopath.

Both are cold and unfeeling in regard to others. They just don't care about anyone but themselves.

Until we can develop a "psychic police" with trustworthy objectivity and powers to arrest and detain those intent on harming others, it's in your own interests to become knowledgeable in this field!

The main problems persons are:

- Criminals
- Borderline Personalities
- Narcissists
- Psychopaths
- Sociopaths

This is not a call to be cruel or dismissive to such people. We all have our motivations but, at rock bottom, we all have the same motivation: to do what we think is the right thing.

The Motivation

The Sly Ones. These troublesome types are intent upon gouging out their path by deliberately undermining other people. They are motivated by hostility or hatred coupled with fear. The former explains their intent to do harm but because of the fear, they cannot attack openly but prefer to be sneaky or "sly" in their machinations.

[These are the people Per Schiøttz said are stuck in some long-gone incident of the past but which they are still fighting. Everything they see in the NOW is an echo of this past battle. The answer is not to try and impose good behavior by force (doesn't work). The effective answer is to locate the hidden struggle of the past and purge it of all emotional charges, so the individual is freed]

The Sly Ones are people characterized as -3 (negative minus 3) on our *Scale Of Emotional Health*. For your own good, you need to familiarize yourself with the chief characteristics of this type. They are very dangerous.

Unfortunately, minus 3s are difficult to spot; only time reveals this trait to individuals higher on the scale as their game strategy unfolds. They always seem to present a cheerful facade, often with a nervous laugh and constant smile. They appear calm, pleasant and resourceful at times.

But inside they are seething.

Through their appearance, words, propaganda or advertising they present themselves, their services or products as being 'so nice, so charming, so condescending and so helpful'. They may seem to be concerned about you, in politely asking probing personal questions about you, your work, your relationships, your sex life, your politics or your religion.

They are storing up ammunition, because they are highly manipulative, they engage in gossip readily but have no qualm in covertly twisting facts around, to knife someone in the back whenever, wherever and to whomever they can.

For objectives that they are too lazy or fearful to undertake themselves, they covertly manipulate and subjugate individuals above and below them on the social scale (Pips) to do their bidding and dirty work.

When confronted, they change the subject to move away from the point and are always rewriting history or changing the truth about past events to suit their current position. They will do and say anything to avoid exposure.

Their targets are any individual, families, tribes, companies or nations that they consider high on the scale and therefore a threat (e.g. +3s, +4s etc.), attempting to "pip" them and bring them down to chronic appeasement, grief and apathy (Minus 4 and Minus 5).

Their *unstated* aim is to cause ruin, discredit achievements and split up relationships. At this they can be very successful and gloat when their victims go down into the lower chronic levels of Minus 4 and 5.

Males at this level subconsciously know their fearful limitations. They can be slothful, but have a need to control and suppress women down to the -4 and -5 levels so that they can feel secure in their sexuality, (also somewhat true of males at -1 and -2).

You could never trust anyone at this level with your health, your money, your reputation, your safety, your husband, your wife, your children, your business, your company, your country, or this planet.

Pips and Pipping

In Supernoetics® we use the term "pips". It means people who shrink or make themselves smaller, under criticism and attack. People dominated by a Sly pips certainly make themselves smaller. If not, they would just tell the oppressor to take a hike!

The Pips do literally limp through life, like cripples. These are your Borderline cases. While ever they are stuck to the Sly that is manipulating them, he or she will never be free and happy. The Sly will effectively see to that.

Borderline Personality Disorder (Emotionally Unstable) is the classic Pip trait; a condition characterized by rapid mood shift, impulsivity, hostility and chaotic social relationships. People with borderline personality disorder usually go from one emotional crisis to another. The wild mood swings are diagnostic: up then down, up again, then down.

For pilots, Pips are a problem, because they appear to be with us and even, at times, seem to do well. They are very pro Supernoetics®. But the Sly has other plans and sooner or later will bring their victim down, unless we take steps with our Freedom Tools to prevent this. If not, the case's setback reflects disastrously on us. You will appear to have failed. You will be blamed...

Sickos. You may recognize this name from Michael Moore's jocular film title for his exposé movie about the US medical care system. "Sicko" is a pun on *Psycho*, the famous 1960 Alfred Hitchcock movie, of course. But by Sickos here, I mean chronically sick people. They need not be crazy (psycho), or borderline, or malingerers, or in any way wanting to be sick. But he or she has definite mental issues, as well as their physical challenges. They are definitely manifesting the "pipping" phenomenon and they must do Per Schiøttz's Freedom Technique to escape, otherwise he or she will never be fully well.

I constantly warn people never to marry, or enter into a long-term relationship with, a chronically sick person. Such an individual has big personal issues and you will inevitably be drawn in. He or she is a Pip.

But a word of caution: *people are often chronically sick because noone knows how to help them.* Depression, anxiety, headaches, inflammations, metabolic disturbances, sexual difficulties, weight disorders and many other chronic conditions may be due to food allergies, chemical overload, nutritional deficiencies and other so-called lifestyle issues. Often there are multiple factors leading to ill health. The person may not really be sick at all, just burdened by toxins!

People with health issues need to clean them up, *before* getting married or starting piloting.

Narcissists. These types are almost as heavy going as The Slies. But the motivation is entirely different. Whereas a Sly wants to harm others and bring them down on purpose, because they are afraid of others being stronger than they are, the narcissist is merely being selfish to the point of stupidity. He or she is looking after self-only and sees others as mere fodder to fulfill their aims. To the card-carrying narcissist, people are tools or devices, even a spouse or lover, set here on Earth to perform services for them alone! It's so logically untenable it makes you want to laugh.

Some narcissists even boast of what they are. He or she is simply blind to the deficiencies in their approach to the game of life. For sure, no narcissist has ever tasted the pleasures of giving or helping others. Their lives are pathetic, thin travesties of engagement.

But be sure, you will find Pips around them or associated with them.

Criminals. Finally, we have the out and out criminal personality. You want nothing to do with these people, if you can avoid it. Never allow one on course or into a piloting situation who is an unreformed criminal (whether caught by the law, or not). They are engaged in taking but not giving. That's the definition of criminal. No matter how much you give, he or she will want more.

A confirmed member of the criminal fraternity is sick inside. He or she is by nature cynical and unhappy. Forget the Hollywood image of the urbane, smart and sophisticated "godfather" mob leader. Such people do not exist in real life. True mobsters have no friends, can trust noone, deal only in death and deprivation and—deep inside, where it counts—he or she knows they are a failed human being. Any one of them would shoot their mother for enough money. Nasty... but true.

Never try to train or pilot a person you know to have criminal tendencies, unless clear evidence of reform is in view (see also Restorative Justice).

We deal instead by those who are crushed, hurt or "pipped" by them.

Are You One Of These Five Types?

If you think you are, you can relax. We all have aspects of these adverse personality traits from time to time. Who has not been naughty, selfish, stupid and destructive towards others, whether intentionally or by accident?

The perfect life has never been lived and may not ever be. We do our best. The criterion is not "Am I bad?" but "Can I put this right?" It's not a question of never making mistakes but putting right the damage, as quickly and effectively as you can. That's the hallmark of sanity and compassion.

In the same vein, be quick to forgive others and forget injuries, especially when someone is trying to make amends. To effect to be "put out", and continuing the huffing and puffing of indignation, is actually rather childish. You are the one likely to suffer most by putting on these play acts.

Moreover, you will not succeed in your intention of making the other person feel wrong.

One of the paramount observations of Transformational Psychology is that noone is ever wrong. He or she will admit afterwards they should not have done it but only because it now makes him or her "right" to own up. In fact justifications are just a way of avoiding being wrong, no matter how injurious the act that was committed.

So knock off the posturing and supercilious claptrap and let the other person have room to screw up. With luck, he or she will do the same for you too!

The Chemical Being

Not quite an adverse personality type—but our world is gradually being taken over by chemicalized zombies: people on Prozac, Zoloft, crack, cocaine, hash, alcohol and sugar/caffeine. Large segments of the population are not real people any more; they are "chemical beings". Their behaviors, responses, attitudes and emotions are being directed by chemical transformation.

Calling this chemical being is, of course, just a joke. It's not at the being end of consciousness and mind; it's down at the animal, biological or what we call "creature" level. Unthinkingness.

It's not a change for the good; far from it. It's a degradation into animal instincts, irrationality and wild behavior, spurred by even wilder emotions. These people are not in control of themselves. How is it possible to police social order and administer justice when you have mainly debased humans who act like madmen and wild animals?

The point is that it makes people very difficult to engage in the matter of social values and compatible behavior. Most of these individuals are out of their minds most of the time; some all of the time. Nothing makes me sadder than to see old video footage of John C. Lilly MD (the dolphin doctor) in his later years. It was a nightmarish picture of a man with a once-brilliant mind who could barely speak intelligibly, his mind mushed by the drugs he had taken.

Ironically, Lilly was a great champion of how good mind-altering drugs are supposed to be, how safe and how everyone should have the freedom to take them (and trash themselves, like he did, presumably). I still recommend his book *The Center Of The Cyclone* in Supernoetics®, not as an instructional aid for what to do but as a guide to what's out there.

Managing Lives

The problem we have with these difficult people—and as you can see there are lots of them—is that their issues overflow into other peoples' lives. They are a liability. That's why I christen them crushers or "adverse" types. We need to have a policy or approach that will protect us, other members the group, while trying to give distraught individuals time and space to sort themselves out.

We don't want to enter into punishment or, even worse, revenge. That's for sick idiots. Here in the USA the childish "justice system" seems hell-bent on extracting revenge, rather than on managing social order. We can do better. But community safety is still the core issue.

Rule one is keep these people at bay. We do not spurn people, stigmatize them or learn to sneer or hate them. But we cannot allow them unfettered access to our organizations and groups, until such a person can self-manage their internal states.

Each difficult type has to deal with their own particular problems, before we can allow them to join us on what is, after all, a major spiritual journey for all. Usually, that means we guide them through a number of steps, an assisted detox, if you like.

The Pips must, of course, unpip themselves. This is not easy. When faced with the reality of the person they have been overwhelmed by, he or she typically wants to disown them, but not without first being abusive and creating a storm. This must be prevented. It solves nothing.

Instead, we use Per Schiøttz's *Freedom Tools Technique*. It's simple to do, permanently effective and can be successful with a beginner (someone "off the street"). We do not insist on so-called disconnection from a crusher or adverse type. Disconnection is vicious, judgmental and unnecessary. What the person needs to disengage from is the act of making self smaller!

See, adverse personality types would have no effect on anybody, if it were not for the tendency of people to seek blame within themselves. "I must be at fault..." So he or she agrees with the criticism and makes self smaller. That's the killer.

But we can fix it with the Freedom Tools.

Note (a technical point): the real hurtful person is sometimes not the person present in the current environment—he or she may only be a reminder or restimulator of the real Sly, who might no longer be alive. Indeed, the real cause of the instability and pipping may even be in a previous life. This is a tricky situation which needs expert handling, only by an advanced pilot with impeccable GSR metering skills.

Notwithstanding, Pips need to get themselves out from under the relevant crusher before they are welcomed back into piloting and school.

Keith Scott-Mumby

For Supernoetics® Inc.

Copyright © 2015 Keith Scott-Mumby ALL RIGHTS RESERVED.

GLOSSARY

Borderline

A personality disorder in which the person is very unstable psychologically, ranging through a wide variety of emotions and impulsive behaviors, most of which are serious over-reactions to the current circumstances. It always has a strong pip element, which is not recognized by orthodox psychologists or psychiatrists.

Capaciousness

The quality of having sufficient capacity of mind to understand and accept other peoples' ideas, principles and beliefs, even though very different from ones own.

Chemical Beings

Individuals whose natural emotional and behavioral responses are blighted and twisted by the use of various chemical modulators, such as marijuana, heroin, crack, alcohol, caffeine, sugar and prescribed medications with complex side-effects. The outcome of this is that such an individual is not really "present", in the full meaning of the word, but dispersed, foggy, distemperate and irrational in varying degrees.

Cultural Pipping

The phenomenon in many cultures and religions, in which the individual is forced, by social norms, to extinguish his or her unique viewpoint but instead accept the consensus thinking. This means, in effect, the individual is required to make him or herself smaller than their own natural dreams, ideals and goals.

Ethical Codex

Everyone has a personalized set of fixed "rules" by which he or she chooses to live. This is not always a fully conscious list of rules; they may be hidden (subconscious). But the individual is driven by them. A moral code is always driven by a set of values which, again, may or may not have been consciously adopted.

Charge, Emotional

Charge is the dark or negative psychic energy enshrined within a bad memory. It's what adds hurtful and unwanted reactions to the present environment. Charge gives rise to unpleasant emotions, negative thoughts, irrationality and unwanted behaviors. We remove it by a special technique we call MINT (make it NOW technique). The memory is then brought to a condition we call "clean and useful", meaning the memory is still there and valid, but it no longer has the potential to cause trouble.

Inner Critic, The

The inner critic or "critical inner voice" is a concept used in popular psychology and psychotherapy to refer to a sub-personality that judges and demeans a person. This voice may be saying phrases like: "You're no good" or "Nobody loves you". It can also be a perfectionist voice, which makes life very demanding, by insisting "Everything must be perfect" or "You must not make a mistake, it will be a disaster."

Narcissist

A narcissist is a wholly and irredeemably selfish person, who believes that other people are there solely to serve him or her. They have grandiose ideas of self-worth. Narcissists are demanding of their every need, yet never help or care for others. The term comes from the legend of Narcissus in Greek mythology, a youth who fell helplessly in love with his own reflection in a pool!

Pilot (Piloting)

Piloting is the term we use in Supernoetics® for Quality Of Life Coaching. It takes place in a one-to-one comfortable environment. The leader, the pilot, asks the client tested and penetrating questions, which sooner or later start releasing charge. The pilot is steering or guiding and this term takes its name from a river boat pilot, who is able to guide and steer the boat to a safe harbor.

Pip

A person who makes him or her self smaller, in response to life situations which call for positive courage and determination, and at which the person failed. Sometimes there is an enforcing agent, whose overbearing presence triggers the pip to shrink. But it's important to grasp that ONLY the pip can make him or herself smaller. The dominator does not do it. This is the opposite of the "victim" mentality (things done TO the person).

Pipping

The process by which a person is persuaded to make him or her self smaller, whether by word, gesture, mannerism or attitude, which implies the pip is no good. Setting up loser situations is also a kind of covert pipping, knowing the individual will fail and so experience a loss of self-worth.

Psychopath

A psychopath is someone with a personality disorder in which they care nothing for the feelings of others. Psychopaths can hurt fellow humans with impunity, not caring, or indeed not even being aware of, what the victim is suffering. A psychopath has no real empathy and numerous studies have shown that the psychopath personality does not even recognize the emotions of others. So, for example, when about to murder someone, the true psychopath is unaware that the facial expression they are seeing denotes real terror.

Sicko (Chronically Sick)

This is a joke expression used by Michael Moore for his film expose of the rotten US health service. He in turn was adapting and twisting its use from the famous 1960 movie by Alfred Hitchcock, *Psycho*. Dr. Keith Scott-Mumby simply adopted this term to describe a person who was chronically sick. Disease does not happen in a vacuum. Chronically sick people have serious psychological injuries, either as the cause of their health problems or, at the very least, as a result of their chronic health suffering. Look up the term *valetudinarian*.

Sociopath

A sociopath is similar to a psychopath, in being cold and unfeeling towards others. A sociopath would not recognize, follow or care about community guidelines or "rules" to protect other society members. A sociopath can't understand others' feelings. They'll often break rules, or make impulsive decisions or enter on destructive actions, without feeling guilty for the harm they cause. Sometimes also known as anti-social personality disorder or ASPD.

Sly

These are the crafty people who seek a solution to their life issues by harming or bringing down others. They operate from a mixture of anger and fear. They want to destroy or harm others but are too fearful to do it out in the open. So they become covert; sneaky. In Per Schiøttz's writings, these people are grasping at freedom as if there was not enough to go round. So to protect themselves—to come out "on top"— they infringe on the freedom of others. The basic motivation of such a person is they are stuck in some past conflict or strife, in which the only way to triumph was to "win" (kill).

A classic literary "Sly" (now a movie) is the character of Grima Worm-tongue, in J R R Tolkein's trilogy, "The Lord of The Rings".

UN-sanity

This is a term coined by Polish Count, American émigré, Alfred Korzybski (1879–1950). He meant the thoughts and actions of a person who was crazy only in certain, limited directions, but not otherwise insane. So a clever and successful businessman might tempt fate by having sexual relations with under-aged girls. He was generally of sound mind but, in respect of this one topic, he was UN-sane.

Utilitarianism

This is the doctrine developed by Jeremy Bentham (1748–1832) and extended by John Stuart Mill (1806–1873), that actions are right if they are useful or for the benefit of a majority. An action is good or worthy insofar as it promotes happiness, and that the greatest happiness of the greatest number should be the guiding principle of conduct.

Anthony Ashley Cooper, the 3rd Earl of Shaftesbury (1671–1713) is generally thought to have been the one of the earliest 'moral sense' theorists, holding that we possess a kind of "inner eye" that allows us to make moral discriminations.

Critics point to the flaw in utilitarianism, that it may be very hard to determine long-term outcomes, and to be sure that there was ultimate benefit for the majority in a particular course of action, not just short-term happiness.

Supernoetics® is a utilitarian philosophy, holding to Anthony Ashley Cooper's precept, that we "know" what's right and wrong at a deeper level and in a broader, fuller context.

Printed in Great Britain
by Amazon

40221824R00061